Writing Micro-Memoirs

Small Stories, Lasting Impact

Kelsey Pearce

Table of Contents

Preface

I've always had a story in my head. Sometimes it's fiction—characters wandering through imaginary streets, conversations that never happened. Sometimes it's a moment from real life, a point in time that replays over and over in my mind until I can almost smell the air and hear the background noises again.

For me, writing has always been the way to make room for more stories. When I put an idea or a memory on paper, it's like unpacking a storage box in my mind. Once it's out, there's space for the next one to arrive.

I've learned that even the simplest events can become a short personal memoir. A neighbour's wave. A dropped ice cream cone. A sentence that someone spoke to you years ago that still lingers. These are the raw materials: planks, nails, and windows of a story.

Writing one down is a lot like building a house room by room. You start with a foundation—a single moment. Then you add walls: a few sensory details, a sprinkle of dialogue, a flash of emotion. Before you know it, you've created a space that the reader can step into. And if you've built it well, they'll feel something when they're there.

This book is my invitation for you to join me in that process—to open the boxes in your mind, unpack the moments, and start building a memory-houses of your own.

Introduction

Why Short Stories Matter

People tend to pay attention when a friend tells a brief, memorable story at a party, but they lose interest and stop listening when the story turns into a fifteen-minute monologue. Sometimes, less really is more.

In a world where our days are divided into notifications, headlines, and scrollable seconds, short-form memoirs fit the way we live and read now. They're the literary equivalent of a perfect espresso shot—concentrated, bracing, and unforgettable. You can read one in the time it takes to stir your tea, yet carry it with you all day.

But don't mistake brevity for shallowness. A well-crafted micro-memoir can hold as much heart as a full-length autobiography. In just a few paragraphs, you can capture an entire friendship, the grief of losing someone you love, or the joy of discovering who you are.

How Micro-Memoirs Differ from Journaling and Essays

Journaling is where you pour everything out for yourself—unedited, unfiltered. It's a private conversation between you and the page.

Essays invite reflection and structure, but they often ask for more background, argument, or explanation. They can feel like opening the door to your living room, inviting the reader to sit down and stay a while.

A micro-memoir? That's a snapshot handed to the reader in the middle of a busy street. It says: Here. This is what I saw. This is what it felt like. Then it lets them fill in the spaces with their own memories.

Who This Book Is For

This is not a book for "writers." It's a book for anyone with a life.

If you've ever told someone, "Oh, let me tell you about the time…" and seen them lean in to listen, you already have the instincts of a memoirist. You don't need a publishing deal, a dramatic life story, or a writing degree. You just need the moments you care about and the willingness to tell them with honesty.

Micro-stories matter because they build the bridge between your life and someone else's. They're how we connect in an era that sprints by for big speeches. And by the time you finish this book, you'll know how to catch those moments, pin them to the page, and let them speak for themselves. This is where the introduction text will go.

This guide is for both writers exploring the craft of micro-memoir and those considering publishing—whether privately, independently, or traditionally.

Part I

The Heart of a Micro-Memoir

Chapter 1

What is a Micro-Memoir?

A micro-memoir is a true story from your life told in about 300 words or fewer—short enough to be read in one sitting, but long enough to carry emotional weight. It's the literary equivalent of a photograph rather than a full-length movie: a single, vivid moment captured in words. Instead of covering years of events, it focuses on a single scene, a pivotal moment, or a key emotional beat.

You've probably written or spoken something like a micro-memoir without realizing it. Think about the times you've told a friend a short story over coffee—a childhood mishap, the way you met your partner, or the day you quit your job. In just a few sentences or paragraphs, you conveyed a beginning, middle, and end, often with a hint of emotion that made it stick. That's the heart of micro-memoir writing.

Why Brevity Works

At first glance, a 300-word limit might seem restrictive, even frustrating. But brevity is one of the micro-memoir's greatest strengths. With limited space, there's no room for digression or filler. You're forced to choose your words with care, to distil a memory down to its essential details and emotions. This focus often results in a story that feels sharper, more immediate, and more powerful than a longer piece.

Brevity also respects the reader's time and attention. In a world of constant distractions and endless content, a well-crafted short piece can cut through the noise. It's a moment of connection that can be absorbed quickly but remembered for a long time.

Think of it as the difference between looking at a single striking photograph versus flipping through an entire album. Both have value, but the single image stays with you because it's concentrated, unblurred by too much context.

Micro-Memoir vs. Full-Length Memoir

While a micro-memoir and a full-length memoir both share the goal of telling true, personal stories, their approaches are vastly different.

A full-length memoir covers a large portion of your life or explores a central theme in depth. It might span decades, weaving in multiple storylines, relationships, and turning points. It has space for a rich backstory, gradual character development, and thematic exploration.

A micro-memoir, by contrast, is a single scene, or a tightly focused narrative. There is no sweeping timeline, no requirement to "start at the beginning." Instead, you drop the reader directly into the most vivid, meaningful moment, and you leave them with an impression, an emotion, or a question that lingers after the last word.

If a memoir is a documentary film, a micro-memoir is a snapshot. Both can move people, but they move them in different ways. One immerses you in the full journey; the other invites you to pause and notice the power of one specific instant. And just like individual photographs can be gathered into a scrapbook, a collection of micro-memoirs can be compiled into a larger manuscript—each piece standing alone while contributing to a bigger story.

The Art of the Slice

The micro-memoir isn't meant to replace longer memoir writing—it's a distinct art form altogether. Some stories require the space of a book; they need a full story arc, but others shine brightest when told in a concentrated form. A single act of kindness from a stranger, a childhood argument with a sibling, the moment you realized you were in love—these experiences don't need chapters to resonate.

In fact, the smallness of a micro-memoir can make it more relatable. Readers see themselves in your moment, not because they lived your exact experience, but because they've felt something similar. In just a few paragraphs, you can create a bridge between your life and theirs.

In the chapters ahead, we'll explore how to choose these moments, shape them into narratives, and use brevity to your advantage. But first, remember this: you don't need a dramatic life story to write a micro-memoir. You just need the courage to notice and the willingness to share.

Chapter 2

Finding Your Voice & Perspective

In a memoir—whether 300 words or 300 pages—your "voice" is your most important tool. Voice is not just how you write; it's how you sound on the page. It's the personality that comes through in your choice of words, your rhythm, your perspective, and even the silences between your sentences, the white space.

Readers don't just want the events of your life—they want you. They want the version of you who tells the story in a way no one else can. That's what makes your work stand out in a sea of personal narratives.

Finding Your Voice

Voice begins with honesty. Not every writer has to sound poetic or literary—some of the most compelling memoirs are written in plain, unadorned language. The key is to lean into your natural way of expressing yourself.

One way to find your voice is to imagine telling your story to a friend. Notice the words you choose, the details you emphasize, and the moments where your tone shifts—whether toward humour, vulnerability, or reflection.

Another way is to study the writers you love. Ask yourself: What is it about their writing that pulls me in? It might be their humour, their directness, their lush imagery, or the way they're willing to be brutally honest. You're not trying to copy them, but you can learn which qualities resonate with you and fold them into your own style.

Making Your Story Stand Out

Many people have lived through similar experiences—childhood friendships, heartbreak, loss, joy, travel, and family drama. What makes your story special is not necessarily the event itself but your unique perspective on it.

Think of two people attending the same wedding. One might focus on the tearful vows and the bride's laugh; another might remember the rainstorm that soaked everyone's shoes. The details you choose to highlight reveal your personality, priorities, and worldview.

- You can also make your story stand out by:
- Zeroing in on specific sensory details instead of general descriptions.
- Allowing your emotional reactions to be as important as the facts.

Offering a surprising angle—perhaps telling the story from the perspective of a bystander, or starting at an unexpected moment.

Writing Conversationally Without Losing Depth

"Write like you talk" is great advice—up to a point. A conversational style makes your writing approachable and authentic, but it's not the same as transcribing everyday speech. In real conversations, we wander, use filler words, and often rely on body language to fill in the gaps. On the page, you need to provide the reader with a bit more.

To strike the right balance:

- Keep your sentences varied in length—short ones for impact, longer ones for reflection.
- Use contractions and casual phrasing where it feels natural, but avoid too much slang that could date your work.
- Imagine you're telling the story to a curious friend, not a formal audience.
- Layer in meaning by choosing words that reflect the emotion behind the moment.

A conversational tone draws readers in; depth is what makes them stay. If your voice carries warmth, wit, honesty, or vulnerability—and pairs it with meaningful observations—you'll create a connection that lasts beyond the final word.

One Story, Three Voices

The way you tell a story can significantly alter how it feels to the reader. The facts stay the same, but the voice—your tone, word choice, rhythm, and emotional focus—shapes the experience.

To show how this works, here's the same true story told three different ways: one in a conversational and humorous voice, one in a poetic and reflective style, and one in a direct, minimalist tone.

As you read, notice:

- Which details are included or left out?
- How sentence length changes the pace.
- How does each version make you feel differently, even though it's the same event?

Conversational & Humorous Voice

I took my teddy bear everywhere. He was more thread than fluff by the time the Easter parade rolled around, but I didn't care—he was perfect. Somewhere between the floats and the candy wrappers, he disappeared.

My parents tried damage control. They bought a brand-new teddy, yanked off the bow, and—right there in the store—stomped him into something they thought passed for "well-loved." I was not fooled. You can't fake history.

Enter our family friend, my knight in flannel armour. He walked the entire parade route, stopping in shop after shop, asking, "Anyone seen a teddy?" Hours later, he found him—faded, limp, and absolutely beautiful.

Teddy sits on a shelf in my bedroom now, forty-five years later. He's not much to look at, but neither am I before coffee. We've both earned our wrinkles.

Word Count: 138

Annotation: Conversation & Humorous Voice

- Uses casual language ("damage control," "knight in flannel armour") to create humour.
- Mixes short and medium sentences for a friendly rhythm.
- Adds asides ("neither am I before coffee") to keep the tone light and relatable.

Poetic & Reflective Voice

Once, I lost my first love at a parade.
He was small, brown, and balding at the seams,
a teddy bear shaped by years of sleep-warm hands.
In the scramble of Easter hats and brass bands,
he slipped away.

My parents brought me another.
They stripped his bow,
ground him underfoot in the store aisle,
tried to bruise him into familiarity.
But grief knows the difference.

A friend of the family
walked the route back,
past melting chocolate bunnies
and paper streamers,
until he found my bear waiting in a shop.

Forty-five years later,
he waits still—
stitched thin,
soft with memory,

patient on a shelf

where my heart can reach him.

Word Count: 112

Annotation: Poetic & Reflective Voice

- Line breaks slow the pace, encouraging the reader to linger on each image.
- Relies on metaphor and sensory language ("sleep-warm hands," "bruise him into familiarity").
- Condenses facts to make room for emotion and imagery.

Direct & Minimalist Voice

I was four. My bear was gone.

We'd been to the Easter parade. I'd dragged him the whole way—past the floats, the music, the candy on the pavement. Somewhere, I dropped him.

My parents bought a new one. Took off the ribbon. Stepped on it. Handed it to me like a magic trick.

It wasn't.

A family friend searched the whole route. Shop to shop. Asking. Looking. He found my bear.

I still have him. Forty-five years later.

Word Count: 79

Annotation: Direct & Minimalist Voice

- Short, clipped sentences give a sense of immediacy and loss.
- Minimal adjectives focus the reader on the bare facts.

- White space and paragraph breaks create emotional pauses.

One Story, Three Voices

Choose a memory—something that happened in less than a day. It could be:

- The moment you learned to ride a bike.
- A time you got caught in the rain without an umbrella.
- The best (or worst) meal you've ever had.

Now, write the same memory three different ways:

Conversational & Humorous: Imagine telling it to a friend over coffee. Use casual language, a little wit, and a tone that invites the reader in.

Poetic & Reflective: Slow down. Focus on imagery, emotion, and rhythm. Let the reader linger on your words.

Direct & Minimalist: Strip the story down to the essentials. Use short sentences. Let the pauses carry weight.

When you're done, read them aloud.

- Which version feels most like you?
- Which one changes how you feel about the memory?
- Which would you want a stranger to read?

Remember: you don't have to choose just one voice for every story. The more you experiment, the more flexible and confident your writing will become.

Voice & Style Checklist

Use this quick guide as you draft and revise your micro-memoirs.

Tone

- ☐ Does the tone match the mood of the story? (serious, playful, reflective, bittersweet)
- ☐ Am I being authentic to my way of speaking, rather than imitating someone else's style?
- ☐ Have I avoided tone shifts that might confuse the reader?

Word Choice

- ☐ Are my words precise and specific rather than vague or generic?
- ☐ Have I removed filler words and clichés that weaken the writing?
- ☐ Do my details reflect my perspective on the event?

Pacing

- ☐ Do my sentence lengths create the rhythm I want—short for tension, longer for reflection?
- ☐ Have I used paragraph breaks or white space to give the reader moments to breathe?
- ☐ Does the story move forward without unnecessary detours?

Connection

- ☐ Have I shown enough detail for the reader to see and feel the moment?

- ☐ Am I revealing something honest or vulnerable that invites empathy?
- ☐ Does my voice make the story feel personal, not just factual?

Intention

- ☐ Do I know why I'm telling this story and what I want the reader to feel?
- ☐ Have I chosen the best voice (conversational, poetic, minimalist, etc.) for that purpose?
- ☐ Does the story sound like me when I read it aloud?

Chapter 3

The Power of Vulnerability

If voice is what makes your writing sound like you, vulnerability is what makes it feel like truth.

We connect with other people through their realness—their quirks, their scars, their stumbles—not through a polished image of perfection. A well-crafted micro-memoir can be beautiful, but if it hides the heart behind a wall of safe generalities, it risks becoming forgettable.

When you share an authentic moment, whether it's an awkward encounter, a heartbreak, or a private joy, you give the reader something to hold on to. They may not have lived your exact story, but they've felt something like it—and that recognition is where connection begins.

Why Emotional Honesty Connects Readers

Readers aren't just looking for events; they're looking for resonance. Emotional honesty creates that resonance.

Think of the times someone told you about their own struggles or fears, and you felt a rush of relief—It's not just me. That's the gift of vulnerability on the page. It doesn't make you weaker; it makes your writing more human.

This doesn't mean you have to expose every detail of your life. You control the lens. You decide how close the reader gets, how much context you offer, and which moments you keep for yourself. Vulnerability is about truth, not total disclosure.

Overcoming Fear of Judgment

One of the hardest parts of writing personal stories is the voice in your head asking, What will people think?

That fear can stop you before you even begin. Here are a few ways to mute it:

- Write for yourself first. Give yourself permission to put everything on the page, knowing you can decide later what to share.
- Remember your "why." You're telling the story to connect, to heal, to preserve, or to inspire—not to please everyone.
- Detach from outcome. Once you release a story, people will interpret it through their own experiences. That's beyond your control—and part of the magic.

If your story involves sensitive topics or people who are still living, you can choose to:

- Change names, places, or identifying details.

- Combine multiple real people into a single composite character.
- Publish anonymously.

We'll cover the ethics and legalities of protecting identity more deeply in Chapter 6, but for now, know that vulnerability doesn't require recklessness. You can be brave and careful.

Writing About Grief, Loss, and Trauma in a Healthy Way (Penning Your Pain)

Some of the most powerful micro-memoirs are born from pain. But writing about grief, loss, or trauma requires care—both for you and your reader.

For yourself:

- Give the story time if you need it. Writing too soon can reopen wounds rather than heal them.
- Consider writing privately first, without the intention of sharing, to process your emotions.
- Recognize when you need to step away from the page and care for yourself in other ways.

For your reader:

- Avoid overwhelming them with raw detail—focus on the emotional truth rather than a blow-by-blow account.
- Balance heaviness with moments of light, hope, or reflection.

- Offer a takeaway: something you learned, something that changed, or simply the acknowledgment that the moment mattered.

When written with care, stories of loss can be as much about resilience as they are about grief. They remind both the writer and the reader that we are not alone in our hardest moments.

Vulnerability in Action

Talking about vulnerability in writing is one thing—seeing it on the page is another. The following micro-memoirs are genuine stories, written with the same principles we've discussed: emotional honesty, selective detail, and respect for both the writer and the reader.

Each one captures a different facet of vulnerability:

- Grief for something longed for but never gained.
- Embarrassment in a moment of unintended self-exposure.
- Joy after years of struggle.

Notice how the emotional tone shapes the language, pacing, and level of detail. A grief story often unfolds slowly, letting emotion build; an embarrassment story might be clipped, matching the speed at which the moment happened; a joy story might linger on the reveal, giving readers time to savour it.

Also, pay attention to what is not said. In memoir, sometimes the spaces between the words—the pauses, the omissions—carry as much power as the sentences themselves.

These are not simply "sad," "awkward," or "happy" stories—they are windows into human experience, told with care so that any reader can step inside, feel something, and carry a piece with them.

Grief—The Life That Wasn't

As a little girl, I always pictured myself as a mother one day—but not a wife. At thirty-four, I decided I wouldn't wait any longer. I began IUI treatments, taking the medications, going through the procedure, and then waiting the required two weeks to find out if it worked.

In the days of waiting, I acted as if I were already pregnant. I spoke words of love to the unconfirmed life inside me, imagined what it would feel like to hold them, even avoided my addiction to diet cola "just in case."

The call came at the office. The nurse's voice was kind but unshakable: You're not pregnant.

I thanked her, hung up, and finished the day without a word to anyone. Only when I shut my car door did I let the tears come. I sobbed until my vision blurred, mourning something that had never existed but had been completely real to me.

Word Count: 155

Annotation: Grief—The Life That Wasn't

- The opening sentence sets expectations: starting with the childhood vision of being a mother establishes a long-held dream, creating emotional stakes before the loss is revealed.

- Specific timeline detail ("at thirty-four") grounds the story in an actual moment, increasing believability.
- The present tense in "I acted as if I were already pregnant" puts the reader inside the waiting period, letting them feel the hope.
- Gentle sensory detail ("spoke words of love", "avoided coffee") conveys tenderness without overloading with description.
- The call scene is brief but powerful: by summarizing the nurse's words rather than dramatizing them, the focus stays on the narrator's reaction, not the dialogue.
- Controlled pacing: withholding tears until the car scene mirrors the narrator's emotional restraint, making the eventual release feel more intense.
- The last sentence ("mourning something that had never existed…") encapsulates the paradox of grief for imagined futures, offering a universal truth that many readers can relate to.

Embarrassment—The Sea Glass Confession

I was in my forties when I learned the truth: sea glass is, quite literally, glass.

We were on a family trip to Prince Edward Island, a day of starfish hunting and shoreline scavenging. The kids raced ahead, buckets in hand, while I lingered behind a small sea glass jewellery shop. An employee joined us on the beach, cheerfully pointing out the glittering fragments at our feet. "This stretch gets a lot," she explained, "because ships used to toss their garbage into these waters."

I froze, blinking at her. Garbage? Broken bottles? Shards of old jars? That was sea glass?

For decades, I had believed otherwise. I knew craft stores sold polished glass pebbles, but I'd assumed that was the imitation version. Real sea glass, I thought, came from the ocean itself—from creatures like jellyfish or Portuguese man-of-war, their bodies hardened into luminous shards after death. Nature's gemstones, not human leftovers.

The realization hit me with the force of a rogue wave. I confessed my misunderstanding out loud, and the poor shop clerk stared at me as if I had grown a second head. I laughed nervously, brushing it off, but inside I burned with embarrassment. How could I, a grown woman, have carried such a childish misconception?

Still, the memory has softened, like the very glass that betrayed me. Now, whenever I hold a piece of sea glass—green, blue, amber—I see both what it is and what I once believed it to be. A little foolishness, a little wonder, smoothed by time and tide into something oddly beautiful.

Word Count: 262

Annotation: Embarrassment—The Sea Glass Confession

- The opening line is a playful confession, immediately drawing readers in with humour and vulnerability.
- Grounding the story in a real setting (Prince Edward Island, scavenging with kids) makes it vivid and believable.
- The misunderstanding (thinking sea glass came from sea creatures) is both embarrassing and endearing, creating relatability.

- Dialogue with the employee highlights the social sting of realizing the mistake.
- The metaphor of a "rogue wave" conveys the shock, while the reflection on life smoothing our edges ties the anecdote to a universal truth.
- The last note turns embarrassment into insight, showing how ordinary misunderstandings can hold lasting meaning.

Joy—Two Fingers or a Peace Sign?

After my first IUI failed, there were more tries. More medications. More blood draws. More disappointments. Six attempts in all.

Then came the IVF cycle—the one I told myself I wouldn't get too attached to, just in case. But the last effort, the whole shebang.

When the doctor called me into his office, I was already bracing for the fateful bad news. Instead, he broke into a smile. You're pregnant. With twins.

I sat in stunned silence for a moment, then walked into the waiting room where my sister was sitting. Speechless, I could only hold up two fingers. Would she understand or think I was giving her an awkward peace sign?

She understood instantly. Tears welled in her eyes, matching mine. This time, they were tears of joy.

Word Count 130

Annotation: Joy-Two Fingers or a Peace Sign?

- The opening contrasts past failure with the present moment. Reminding the reader of multiple failed attempts heightens the emotional payoff.
- Repetition (more medications, more blood draws, more disappointments) creates rhythm and reinforces the relentlessness of the journey.
- Short, direct sentences in the lead-up (Then came the IVF cycle…) slow the pacing, building suspense before the news is revealed.
- Dialogue choice (You're pregnant. With twins.) is concise and high impact, allowing the reader to feel the emotional whiplash.
- Nonverbal reveal (I could only hold up two fingers) adds cinematic quality and communicates joy without spelling it out.
- Ending on shared tears creates connection and resonance—this joy is not private but witnessed, making it more powerful for the reader.

Writing Your Emotional Micro-Memoir

Choose one moment from your life that stirred a powerful emotion—grief, joy, embarrassment, pride, fear, or relief. It doesn't have to be the biggest moment of your life; sometimes the smallest experiences hold the deepest feelings.

Step 1—Choose Your Emotion

Decide which emotion you want to focus on. This will guide your tone, pacing, and detail.

Step 2—Capture the Core Scene

In a few bullet points, jot down:

- Where were you?
- Who was with you (if anyone)?
- What happened?
- How did you feel at that moment?
- How do you feel looking back now?

Step 3—Write the First Draft

Write the story in 300 words or fewer. Keep the focus tight—one scene, one emotion.

Step 4—Edit for Emotional Clarity

Ask yourself:

- Am I being emotionally honest, or am I holding back?
- Have I included enough sensory detail to make the reader feel it?
- Is there anything I can remove that distracts from the core emotion?

Step 5—Protect Yourself and Others

If necessary, modify names, alter identifying details, or create a composite character. Vulnerability doesn't mean sacrificing privacy.

Bonus Challenge:

Once your story is done, try rewriting it in a different emotional tone. For example, if it's grief, see if you can tell it with a thread of humour; if it's joy, try telling it in a restrained, minimalist style. You may discover new angles on the same memory.

Emotional Lens Reference

This Emotional Lens Reference is your shortcut to shaping the tone of your micro-memoir. Once you know the core emotion you want to convey, use the bullet points to guide your choices. Let the word choice shape the feel of your sentences, let the pacing control the reader's heartbeat, and use imagery to anchor the emotion in a tangible scene. By adjusting all three, you can make the reader feel the way you did—whether it's the slow ache of grief, the light-saturated joy of success, or the quick sting of embarrassment.

Grief

- Word Choice: soft, muted language; metaphors of absence or fading
- Pacing: slower; allows emotion to build gradually
- Imagery: shadows, dim light, stillness, endings

Joy

- Word Choice: bright, vivid words; sensory images that sparkle
- Pacing: Lingering; savouring moments and details
- Imagery: bright, colourful, warmth, open space

Embarrassment

- Word Choice: self-deprecating humour; sharp, quick phrasing

- Pacing: fast; mimics the quick burn of the moment
- Imagery: awkward gestures, flushed cheeks, misplaced focus

Fear

- Word Choice: urgent, tense words; sensory cues of danger
- Pacing: quick, clipped sentences; builds suspense
- Imagery: darkness, sudden movement, sounds that spike awareness

Pride

- Word Choice: confident, affirming language; metaphors of strength
- Pacing: steady and balanced; matches feeling of accomplishment
- Imagery: sunrise, climbing, strong structures

Relief

- Word Choice: gentle, calming words; imagery of release and openness
- Pacing: smooth and unhurried; mirrors exhale after tension
- Imagery: gentle breezes, setting down burdens, open doors

Part II

The Craft of Telling It Well

Chapter 4

Structure in Miniature

A micro-memoir may be small, but it still needs structure. Without it, even the most heartfelt story can feel scattered or incomplete. In under 300 words, you don't have space for detours—you need a clear beginning, middle, and end, each pulling the reader forward.

Think of your story like a paper airplane: every fold matters. Get the angles right, and it will soar. Rush the folds, and it will flop.

How to Create a Narrative Arc in Under 300 Words

Even short stories need a journey. In a micro-memoir, the arc is tight but still recognizable:

1. **Set the scene quickly.** Who's there? Where are we? What's happening? Provide the reader with just enough information to get oriented.
2. **Introduce the tension or change.** Something shifts—a decision, an event, a discovery, an emotion.

3. **Offer resolution or reflection.** End with what changed (or didn't) because of that moment.

Example Structure in 3 Sentences:

- *Beginning:* "At seven, I thought the neighbour's pool was the ocean."
- *Middle:* "One summer day, I waded in and realized the bottom was only three feet away."
- *End:* "It took me twenty years to learn that all the oceans I feared were shallower than I thought."

In longer memoirs, you can wander into subplots or backstory. In micro-memoirs, every sentence must push the arc forward.

Show, Don't Tell in Short Prose

"Show, don't tell" matters even more when your word count is tight. Telling says *I was nervous.* Showing says, *my hands slipped twice on the doorknob before I turned it.*

In micro-memoirs:

- Use sensory details to create immediacy. What could you see, hear, smell, or touch in that moment?
- Include specific actions that reveal emotion without naming it.
- Trust the reader to connect the dots—you don't have to explain everything.

The trick is balance. With too much detail, you run out of room for the story; with too little, the emotion disappears.

Crafting an Impactful Opening Line

Your first sentence is the door into your story. A 300-word piece must capture the reader's attention instantly.

Strong openings often:

- Start in the middle of the action: By the time the cake collapsed, my mother had already lit the candles.
- Make a surprising statement: I learned how to lie the summer my grandfather taught me poker.
- Create curiosity or tension: The last time I saw her, she was carrying a jar of pickles.

A good opening doesn't have to explain everything—it just has to make the reader want to keep going. In short prose, curiosity is your greatest hook.

Structure in Action

It's one thing to talk about beginnings, middles, and ends—it's another to see them at work. The following three micro-memoirs each tell a different story: one of travel gone wrong, one of a child's language quirk, and one of a forest adventure with a painful twist. While the topics vary, they all share the same backbone: a clear narrative arc, vivid "showing" details, and an opening line that invites the reader in. As you read, look for how each story wastes no time setting the scene, builds to a shift or turning point, and closes with either resolution or reflection.

From Platform 19 to Platform 2

The rain was torrential when we arrived in Edinburgh. Two adults, two thirteen-year-olds, and four large suitcases—none of which could be left behind—had to get from the airport to the train station. Not because we needed a train, but we were storing our luggage before a bus trip the next morning.

A taxi dropped us at the curb, unloading our suitcases in a no-stopping zone. Down, up, and down the escalators we went, searching for platform 19. On the last downward trip, my soaked pant leg dragged across the metal stairs and was swallowed by the teeth of the escalator. A stranger pulled me free, leaving my pants tattered and my dignity frayed.

We finally found platform 19—in rubble, under construction. The storage centre had moved to platform 2, and from 19 to 2, soaked through and dragging luggage, felt like a marathon.

Word Count: 146

Annotations: From Platform 19 to Platform 2

- Structure: Clear arc—arrival and problem → complication (pants caught) → twist ending (wrong platform).
- Showing, not telling: "Soaked pant leg dragged" and "teeth of the escalator" give vivid sensory detail without saying, "I was wet and frustrated."
- Impactful opening: Starts mid-action with "The rain was torrential," immediately setting tone and stakes.
- Compression: Unnecessary travel details are trimmed to keep momentum.

"Booky"

My son's vocabulary was growing fast—or maybe at the same speed as every other healthy child, but to me it felt like magic. I taught him the word "book," and he clutched one in his small hands, declaring it "booky" with delight.

I wasn't concerned—at first. But over the next few weeks, everything became "booky." The dog was booky. Mama was booky. Even his bottle was booky.

Now he's fourteen, with a vocabulary that could rival a spelling bee champion. But for a short while, I worried the only word he'd ever say was "booky."

Word Count: 97

Annotations: "Booky"

- Structure: Simple three-beat arc—learning the word → overuse becomes a worry → reassurance in hindsight.
- Showing, not telling: Repetition of "booky" lets the reader hear the humour and mild concern without explanation.
- Impactful opening: Starts with a warm, relatable observation that immediately draws parents (and anyone who's been a child) in.
- Tone: Light and affectionate, letting personality shine.

The Log that Buzzed Version 1

The cottage was our place for adventures—some we sought, others found us.

One bright afternoon, siblings and cousins wandered into the forest. My youngest sister and a cousin sat on a log, unknowingly disturbing a wasp nest. The wasps did not appreciate the intrusion. They attacked, tangling in our hair and stinging again and again.

My sister screamed, mouth open, giving one wasp the perfect opportunity to sting inside.

We rushed to the tiny hospital—a familiar stop for this crew of daredevils. We survived, but went straight for ice cream afterward, because even swollen faces deserved dessert.
Word Count: 99

Annotations: The Log that Buzzed Version 1

- Structure: Strong arc—peaceful start → sudden danger → humorous, comforting resolution.
- Showing, not telling: "Tangling in our hair" and "stinging again and again" create vivid discomfort without stating "it hurt."
- Impactful opening: The short first sentence sets up a sense of place and nostalgia before the incident.
- Balancing tone: The story blends danger with humour, keeping it engaging without minimizing the sting (literally).

Let's rewrite the last micro-memoir by moving the end to the beginning.

The Log That Buzzed Version 2 Start at the end

Ice cream is really the best medicine, at least for wasp stings. At least, that's how it felt when we marched from the hospital straight to the parlour, swollen faces grinning over cones.

The cottage had always been our place for adventures—some invited, others ambushing us. One bright afternoon, siblings and cousins wandered into the forest. My youngest sister and a cousin sat on a log, unknowingly disturbing a wasp nest.

The wasps did not appreciate the intrusion. They attacked, tangling in our hair, stinging again and again. My sister screamed, mouth wide, giving one wasp the perfect chance to sting inside.

We survived, as we always did, and the strange logic of childhood ruled: pain earned ice cream. And somehow, dessert made the danger just another story worth retelling.
Word Count: 131

Annotation: The Log That Buzzed Version 2 Start at the end

- Playful Hook: The new first line ("Ice cream is really the best medicine, at least for wasps") immediately blends humour with intrigue, pulling the reader into a story that will balance sting and sweetness.

- Tone Setting: By starting with the cure before the injury, the piece establishes levity, reducing the sting's severity and highlighting resilience.

- Foreshadowed Resolution: The mention of ice cream upfront makes the hospital visit and stings feel like steps toward the real punchline—the shared ritual of recovery.

- Shifted Emphasis: The focus is less on the chaos of the wasp attack and more on how the family coped, reframing the memory as one of bonding rather than fear.

Micro-Memoir Structure Cheat Sheet

Beginning—Set the Scene Quickly

- Who is there?
- Where are we?
- What's happening *right now*?
- Use a detail or action to pull the reader in immediately.

Middle—The Shift

- Introduce the change, tension, or turning point.
- Show how the moment feels through action and sensory details.
- Keep the focus on the core scene—avoid side stories.

End—Resolution or Reflection

- Show what changed because of the moment (or what didn't).
- Offer a final image, line, or insight that lingers in the reader's mind.
- Make sure the ending feels connected to the beginning, even if it's surprising.

Building Your 300-Word Arc

Pick a moment from your life—something that happened in a single day or less. It can be dramatic or ordinary, as long as it mattered to you.

Step 1—Outline the Arc

Write one sentence for each part of your story:

- Beginning: Set the scene—who, where, and what's happening.
- Middle: The shift—what changes, challenges, or surprises occur?
- End: Resolution or reflection—what's different because of this moment?

Step 2—Show, Don't Tell

For each sentence, replace any "telling" words (sad, happy, nervous) with sensory details or actions that let the reader feel it.

Step 3—Hook Them Early

Experiment with three different

opening lines for the same story:

- One that drops the reader into the middle of the action.
- One that makes a surprising or intriguing statement.
- One that creates curiosity with an unusual image or detail.

Step 4—Draft and Trim

Expand your outline into a full micro-memoir of 300 words or fewer. Remove anything that doesn't move the story forward or deepen the emotional impact.

Step 5—Read Aloud

Read your story out loud. Does it move smoothly from start to finish? Does the ending feel connected to the beginning? If not, adjust until it does.

Chapter 5

Capturing Character & Context

In a micro-memoir, you don't have the luxury of a long introduction to each person or place. Bring them to life quickly—often in just a few sentences—while still giving the reader enough context to understand why this moment matters. It's a balancing act: too little, and the story feels flat; too much, and you run out of space for the actual moment.

Bringing People to Life in a Few Sentences

When you introduce a person in a micro-memoir, you want the reader to see, hear, and feel their presence instantly. That doesn't mean listing their height, hair colour, and wardrobe—it means choosing details that reveal personality, mood, and role in the story.

Example:

Telling: "My grandfather was a kind man who loved gardening."

Showing: "Grandpa's hands were permanently stained with soil, and he spoke to his tomatoes as if they were old friends."

See how the second version doesn't just describe him—it puts you in his world and hints at his warmth without saying "kind."

When deciding what details to include:

- Focus on what's unique about them in this moment.
- Use specific actions or quirks that show personality.
- Consider how they speak—one sharp line of dialogue can reveal as much as a paragraph of description.

If cultural or historical context matters—such as family traditions, regional accents, or generational attitudes—choose one or two precise details that anchor the reader without turning the story into a history lesson.

Setting the Scene Without Overloading with Details

The reader needs to know where and when they are, but in a micro-memoir, you can't afford to paint every leaf on the tree. Think of your setting as a stage set—enough to make it believable, but not so much that it distracts from the action.

Tips for scene-setting in short prose:

- Anchor the reader with one strong visual: "The diner's red vinyl booths stuck to the backs of our legs."
- Sprinkle in sensory clues—a smell, a sound, the quality of the light.

- Let the setting interact with the character: rain dripping off an umbrella, gravel crunching underfoot, a chair that wobbles with every shift.
- If the setting is culturally significant (a religious festival, a rural farm, a bustling market), weave in one authentic detail that signals its importance without pausing to explain it in full.

Finding the Balance

In micro-memoirs, character and context should feel woven into the story, not bolted on at the beginning. One way to check: read your piece and highlight every word that's pure description. If you removed it, would the story still make sense? If so, consider trimming it or folding it into action or dialogue.

Quick Portraits and Places

You don't need a full biography or a panoramic landscape to bring someone—or somewhere—alive in a micro-memoir. Sometimes, a single sensory detail or a subtle quirk is enough to make a character memorable or a setting vivid. The goal is to give the reader just enough to step into the moment with you, without slowing the story to a crawl. Here are a few quick sketches of people and places, each built from only two or three sentences, to show how you can capture personality or atmosphere in a flash.

My Father

We could always tell if my father was home. The cracking of his ankles after a long day at work echoes from downstairs. Whether he'd had a good day or a bad one was measured by his breathing—if he huffed, we knew to give him a longer transition time.

Word Count: 50

Annotation: My Father

- Uses a distinctive sound ("cracking of his ankles") as the identifying feature, which instantly personalizes him.
- The breathing as an emotional barometer reveals mood without directly saying, "he was tired" or "he was grumpy."
- Small domestic details make him feel real and familiar to the reader.

My Great-Grandmother

Even in her late nineties, her smile was warm and inviting. The skin on her hands was thin as tissue paper, the blue veins like rivers we could trace with a fingertip. It should have been unsettling, but to my child's eyes, her warmth made age feel safe.

Word Count: 48

Annotation: My Great-Grandmother

- Uses sensory touch imagery ("thin as tissue paper") to evoke age without long explanation.
- Contrasts what "should" be unsettling with the narrator's emotional reality, adding depth.
- The detail of tracing veins adds intimacy and shows the relationship rather than stating it.

The Public Swimming Pool

The waft of chlorine reached us before we saw the building. Inside, the air was warm and thick, a promise of aquatic fun. The echo of splashes and shouts made it impossible to stand still for long.

Word Count: 37

Annotation: The Public Swimming Pool

- Opens with smell before sight, pulling the reader into the scene through a strong sensory cue.
- The "warm and thick" air adds a tactile atmosphere that complements the smell.
- The soundscape (splashes and shouts) completes the multi-sensory setting in just a few words.

Quick Character & Setting Formula

For a Character:

- ☐ Who—Identify them in relation to you or the story (e.g., "my father," "my great-grandmother," "the lifeguard").
- ☐ Defining Detail—Pick one unique feature, quirk, or habit that makes them instantly recognizable.
- ☐ Sensory Anchor—Use sight, sound, touch, smell, or taste to make the description vivid.
- ☐ Emotional Layer—Show how you feel about them or how they make you feel in that moment.

For a Setting:

- ☐ Where & When—Place the reader immediately (e.g., "the public swimming pool on a summer afternoon").

- ☐ Sensory Snapshot—Choose one or two strong sensory cues (smell of chlorine, echo of splashes).
- ☐ Mood or Promise—Hint at what the place means or what's about to happen (e.g., "a promise of aquatic fun").
- ☐ Interaction—Show how people engage with the place (dragging feet through sand, leaning against a railing).

Now Your Turn

Quick Sketches That Stick

Use the formula below to create one quick character introduction and one quick setting snapshot. Keep each under three sentences.

Character Template:

1. **Who:** "My ____________" or "The ____________ I met…"
2. **Defining Detail:** "…was known for ____________" (a quirk, habit, or feature).
3. **Sensory Anchor:** "You could always tell by ____________" (sound, smell, touch, sight).
4. **Emotional Layer:** "It made me feel ____________" or "It told me ____________ about them."

Example:

"Our mail carrier was known for carrying not just letters, but dog treats in his pockets. You could always tell he'd made his rounds by the chorus of joyful barks spilling down the street. Then one day, someone new took over the route—and the cheerful chorus turned back into ordinary alarms. It made me realize how small kindnesses can change the sound of a whole neighbourhood."

Setting Template:

1. **Where & When:** "The ____________ (place) on ____________ (time/season/day)."
2. **Sensory Snapshot:** "It smelled of ____________ and sounded like ____________."
3. **Mood or Promise:** "It promised ____________" or "It felt like ____________."
4. **Interaction:** "We ____________" (action that connects people to the space).

Example:

"The German bakery in the early morning smelled of warm yeast and butter, and the ovens hummed softly. It promised soft rolls and crusty loaves to start the day. We lingered there on our holiday mornings, knowing grocery-store bread at home could never compete."

Challenge:

Write two new quick sketches—one person, one place—based on memories. Read them aloud and ask:

- Can someone who's never met this person picture them?
- Can someone who's never been to this place imagine it?

Bonus Twist: Merge Them into a Scene

Once you've written your quick character and setting sketches, combine them into a single opening paragraph for a micro-memoir. Your goal is to place the character *inside* the setting so the reader experiences both at once.

These are illustrative fictional examples—they're not real memoirs, but they show how you can merge a person and place into an opening that immediately sets the tone. Notice how each uses the same basic structure but creates a different mood.

Formula:

1. Introduce the character with their defining detail or quirk.
2. Anchor them in the setting with a sensory clue.
3. Let the setting influence their mood, actions, or your perception of them.

Funny:

"Aunt Marlene wore her wide-brimmed gardening hat even inside the grocery store. The produce section's misting system had just kicked on, beading water on the lettuce and cooling the air, but she was already fanning herself with a coupon flyer. She said the store had the 'coldest grapes in town,' and she intended to test the claim personally."

Poignant:

"Mr. Harris always arrived at the park bench before the sun cleared the trees. The frost on the grass crunched under his cane, and he placed a single thermos of coffee on the empty space beside him. He never drank from it until the church bells rang at nine."

Tense:

"Leo's leg bounced as he gripped the steering wheel, eyes flicking to the diner's fogged windows. The smell of burnt coffee hit us when the door swung open, but he didn't notice—he was too busy scanning for the man in the red cap. The one who had promised answers."

Your Turn:

- Take your character sketches from earlier and drop them into your setting sketch.
- Adjust so that their quirks and mood interact naturally with the environment.
- Keep it under 80 words—just enough to set the stage for your micro-memoir.

Chapter 6

Turning Life Into Literature

Writing a memoir—or even a short-form personal piece—is more than simply recording what happened. It's about shaping real-life events into something that resonates with readers. That means making choices: what to include, what to leave out, how to balance light and heavy moments, and how to navigate the sometimes tricky waters of truth, privacy, and legality.

Selecting What to Include (and Leave Out)

Not every detail from your life needs to make it onto the page. In fact, the power of memoir often comes from what's *not* said—what's implied, left to the reader's imagination, or simply unnecessary to tell the core story.

When deciding what to include:

- Serve the story, not the scrapbook. Choose moments that advance a theme or emotional arc.

- Trim repetitions. If you've already shown your resilience in one scene, you may not need three more examples.
- Ask: does this add meaning? If a detail doesn't reveal something new about the character, situation, or tone, consider cutting it.

When deciding what to leave out:

- Remove unrelated tangents that slow momentum.
- Skip the backstory unless it deepens the reader's understanding of *this* moment.
- Avoid including private information that isn't yours to share—unless you've weighed the ethical and legal implications.

Balancing Humour and Tragedy in Personal Narratives

Life isn't neatly divided into "funny chapters" and "sad chapters." Often, the moments that stick with us are the ones that mix the two—where a flash of humour cuts through grief, or a poignant moment sneaks into a cheerful scene. This balance makes your story feel more authentic and more relatable.

Tips for mixing tones:

- Let humour arise naturally from character quirks or the situation, not forced jokes.
- Use humour to create relief after a heavy moment, but don't undercut the emotional weight.

- In tragedy, small details of kindness or absurdity can keep the story from feeling one-note.

  Example:

  Tragic: "The funeral home smelled faintly of lilies."

Balanced: "The funeral home smelled faintly of lilies, but the coffee machine in the corner sputtered so loudly it made Aunt Ruth jump every time."

Protecting Privacy in Memoir Writing

Sharing your story doesn't mean you have to expose every real-life detail. You can protect identities, reduce legal risks, and still keep your writing compelling by making thoughtful adjustments.

1. Change Identifying Details

- Names: Swap for new ones with a distinct sound, length, or cultural background.
- Locations: Use a different city, town, or even change urban to rural (or vice versa).
- Dates: Use approximate timeframes ("late summer," "around the holidays") instead of exact dates.

Example:

Original: In June 2015, I saw Mark outside the Denver courthouse.

Anonymized: One summer, I saw a friend outside a downtown courthouse.

2. Merge or Composite Characters

- Combine traits from two or more real people into one fictionalized character.
- Adjust relationships—turn a co-worker into a neighbour, or a sibling into a cousin.
- Change age, occupation, or appearance while keeping the emotional truth intact.

Benefit: It maintains narrative impact while reducing recognizability.

3. Shift the Setting

- Change the environment without altering the core event.
- Move a conversation from the workplace to a park bench, or from a dinner table to a coffee shop.
- Alter small visual cues so the place feels different to outsiders.

4. Alter Physical or Behavioural Traits

- Change height, hair colour, or mannerisms.
- Give them a distinct style of clothing or speech pattern.
- Adjust their hobbies, pets, or favourite sayings.

5. Be Careful with Sensitive Content

- Avoid revealing medical diagnoses, legal troubles, or financial struggles unless you have permission.

- Use general descriptors rather than specifics ("a health scare" vs. "stage II breast cancer" if anonymity is needed).
- If you must share, strip away identifying markers that could link the person directly.

6. When in Doubt—Ask or Invent

- Ask for consent before sharing personal details.
- If consent isn't possible, fictionalize enough that no reasonable reader could identify the person.

Pro Tip: Changing one or two details isn't always enough—layer multiple changes to ensure anonymity. And if the story involves high stakes (legal, emotional, or reputational), consider consulting a publishing lawyer before you release it. See chapter 15 for more information.

Memoir Risk Assessment Checklist

Use this checklist before you publish or share your memoir publicly. It will help you catch potential ethical, emotional, and legal issues.

Ethical Considerations

- ☐ Have I shared only what serves the story's purpose?
- ☐ Have I avoided including private information that isn't mine to tell?
- ☐ Have I considered how others in the story might feel reading this?
- ☐ Have I changed names, locations, or details to protect privacy where needed?

- ☐ If possible, have I asked permission from people portrayed in a sensitive light?

Emotional Readiness

- ☐ Am I ready for strangers (and people I know) to read this?
- ☐ Have I processed enough of the emotions behind this story to handle potential criticism?
- ☐ Could publishing this piece damage important relationships—and am I prepared for that?
- ☐ If feedback is negative, will I regret sharing this?

Side-by-Side: Protecting Privacy in Practice

Original (Unaltered)

On June 12, 2018, I stood outside the red brick courthouse in downtown Asheville, clutching my phone. Mark—still in his grease-stained mechanic's uniform—leaned against the hood of his cherry-red '67 Mustang, smoking like he had all the time in the world. We hadn't spoken in three years, not since he disappeared the day before our wedding. Now, seeing him there, hair longer and eyes just as sharp, I felt every ounce of that old betrayal.

Anonymized (Altered for Privacy)

One summer afternoon, I found myself outside a weathered public building in a small Southern city, holding my phone like a lifeline. A man I used to know leaned against the hood of an old sports car, a cigarette curling smoke into the warm air. We hadn't spoken in years, not since he vanished days before a major milestone in my life. Now, watching him from across the street, I felt the weight of a betrayal that hadn't faded.

What Changed (and Why)

In this example, several items were changed. Not every detail needs to be removed; it depends on the context.

- Specific Date Removed: June 12, 2018 → One summer afternoon to make it less traceable.
- Location Generalized: Downtown Asheville → a small Southern city.
- Identifying Details Altered:
    - Red brick courthouse → weathered public building (removes unique architectural identifier).
    - Mark → A man I used to know (no name given).
    - Mechanic's uniform" omitted profession to reduce recognizability.
    - Cherry-red '67 Mustang" old sports car (removes collectible-specific clue).
- Relationship Context Softened: Day before our wedding → days before a major milestone in my life to conceal event specifics.
- Emotional Core Preserved: The betrayal, shock, and vivid sensory imagery (smoke, heat, distance) remain intact.

The Anonymization Challenge

Your task is to take a short, vivid memory from your life and rewrite it in a way that protects the identities of the people and places involved—without losing the emotional impact.

Step 1 – Write the Original

Write 4–6 sentences describing the memory in rich detail.

- Include specific names, dates, locations, appearances, and dialogue.
- Use all five senses to make it feel real.

Step 2 – Identify Red Flags

Highlight any details that could make someone easily identifiable:
Names

- ☐ Specific dates or times
- ☐ Exact locations
- ☐ Job titles or uniforms
- ☐ Unique possessions (cars, pets, clothing)
- ☐ Specific events or circumstances

Step 3 – Make the Changes

Rewrite your memory by:

- Swapping out names for general descriptors.
- Changing dates to seasons or vague time frames.

- Generalizing or altering location details.
- Adjusting unique characteristics (hair colour, type of car, occupation).
- Soften event specifics while keeping the emotional truth.

Step 4 – Compare & Evaluate

Read both versions side by side. Ask yourself:

- Does the revised version protect identities?
- Does it still carry the same emotional weight?
- Would a stranger still find it compelling?

Pro Tip: If you're unsure whether your revision hides someone's identity enough, imagine them reading it—or imagine their neighbour reading it. If either could easily recognize them, revise again.

Chapter 7

Smaller Than Small — The Power of Ultra-Short Memoirs

Sometimes, the most memorable stories aren't sprawling essays or even full micro-memoirs—they're a single, distilled breath on the page. These ultra-short forms demand precision, creativity, and trust in the reader's imagination. They live in the space between what is said and what is left unsaid.

The Single-Sentence Story

A single-sentence memoir can compress an entire relationship, event, or transformation into one unforgettable line.

Examples:

- *We met, we married, we drifted, we waved.*
- *I sold the house, but the mailbox still has my name.*
- *Mom taught me to swim; I taught her to float.*

Techniques to Try:

- Compression: Strip away every word that isn't essential.
- Implication: Let the reader fill in the blanks. (In *We met, we married, we drifted, we waved,* years of emotional change are implied.)
- White Space: Give the sentence room on the page—no clutter, no explanation, just the line.

Memoir Poetry

Poetry can convey a memoir's emotional truth while embracing rhythm, repetition, and imagery. Unlike prose, it doesn't have to follow a narrative structure—it can be a fragment, a feeling, or a flash.

Forms to Try:

- **Free Verse:** No strict rhyme or rhythm, just distilled emotion and imagery.
- **Found Poetry:** Rearrange words from old letters, journal entries, or even headlines that connect to your memory.
- **Six-Word Memoirs:** Inspired by the famous Hemingway example: *For sale: baby shoes, never worn.*

Examples:

Free Verse:

The kitchen smelled of cinnamon,
your hands of garlic and rosemary,

and I didn't know
it was the last time we'd cook together.

Six-Word Memoir:

Met late. Loved fast. Lost faster.

Haiku for Human Moments

A haiku traditionally follows a 5–7–5 syllable structure, evoking nature. But here, we can adapt it for personal storytelling—tiny snapshots of human experience.

Example:

Dad's old leather coat
still smells of wood smoke and rain.
I keep it hidden.

Why Constraints Work:

The 17-syllable limit forces you to focus on one precise image or moment. That precision sharpens emotion.

When to Go Ultra-Short

Ultra-short memoirs work best when:

- The moment is too fragile for long prose. Some memories lose power if over-explained.
- You want a keepsake or caption. These forms are suitable for inscriptions, social media, or tattoo-worthy lines.
- You want to spark curiosity. A short line can open a space for the reader's imagination.

- High-impact opener: Use as a hook for a longer narrative, foreshadowing the story to come.

Ultra-Short Memoir Techniques

A quick-reference guide for turning big memories into small masterpieces.

1. Compression — The Art of Saying Less

- Cut modifiers unless they add meaning. ("A warm June evening" → "June evening" if warmth is not key.)
- Remove side characters unless they're essential.
- Keep only the emotional core and one or two striking images.

Example: Original: "It was a warm June evening when we sat in the backyard talking about college, your hand tapping the armrest."

Compressed: "In June, you tapped the chair and we talked about leaving."

2. Implication — Let the Reader Fill the Gaps

- Skip the "and then" details. Let one image imply the rest.
- Use contrast to hint at change.
- Focus on the *moment before* or *after* the event for subtlety.

Example: "We met, we married, we drifted, we waved." → implies decades in eight words.

3. White Space — Give It Breathing Room

- Place the single sentence on its own line or page.
- Avoid over-explaining before or after; let it stand alone.
- White space gives the reader time to feel the weight of the line.

4. Poetic Devices for Power

- Repetition: Creates rhythm and emphasis ("You left the cup. You left the keys. You left.").
- Metaphor: Makes the abstract tangible ("Our silence was a locked door.").
- Sound: Alliteration or internal rhyme can make lines linger.

5. Sharpening Imagery

- Choose specific nouns and strong verbs.
- Avoid vague language—replace "thing" with "guitar," "went" with "stumbled."
- One vivid detail can carry the entire piece.

Quick Ultra-Short Checklist

- ☐ Does every word earn its place?
- ☐ Does the image imply more than it says?
- ☐ Can a reader feel the emotion without extra explanation?
- ☐ Could it standalone on a page and still resonate?

From Big to Bare Bones: The Reduction Ladder

One of the most powerful skills in ultra-short memoir writing is learning how to distil a memory without losing its emotional weight. In this exercise, we'll start with a full 300-word micro-memoir and gradually shrink it—first to 50 words, then to a single sentence, and finally to a haiku. The goal isn't to strip the story until it's lifeless; it's uncovering the heartbeat at its core—the one image or emotion that can standalone and still move a reader. To illustrate how it works, we'll use a true childhood story and walk you through it step by step.

Step 1 – The 300-Word Version

I took my teddy bear everywhere. He was the first thing I reached for when I woke up and the last thing I clutched before sleep. By the time the Easter parade rolled around that year, his fur was worn to a thin fuzz, his seams stretched, and his button eyes just a little loose. He smelled faintly of the grass I'd dragged him through and the cookies I'd eaten with him propped in my lap. To me, he was perfect.

Somewhere between the brass bands, the floats throwing candy, and the crowds pressed along the sidewalks, he disappeared. I didn't notice at first. But when I reached for him and my hands met empty air, my stomach dropped. We searched under benches, between folding chairs, even inside the stroller pockets. No teddy.

My parents tried damage control. At the nearest toy store, they bought a brand-new teddy bear—bright-eyed, plush, with a satin bow at his neck. They yanked off the bow and—right there in the aisle—stomped him into something they thought passed for "well-loved." I wasn't fooled. You can't fake history.

Enter our family friend, my knight in flannel armour. He walked the entire parade route backwards, stopping in shop after shop. "Anyone seen a teddy?" He'd ask, holding up his hands as if to cradle an invisible bear. Hours later, he found him—faded, limp, one ear hanging by a thread, and absolutely beautiful.

Now Teddy sits on a shelf in my bedroom, forty-five years later. His seams are fragile, his fabric thin. He's not much to look at, but neither am I before coffee. We've both earned our wrinkles.

Step 2 – 50-Word Version

At the Easter parade, my teddy vanished. My parents tried replacing him with a "well-loved" impostor, but you can't fake history. A family friend retraced the parade route, asking shopkeepers, "Anyone seen a teddy?" Hours later, he returned the faded, limp bear to my arms—perfect, just as he was.

Step 3 – Single Sentence

A friend found my lost teddy after the Easter parade and returned him—faded, limp, and perfect.

Step 4 – Haiku

Easter crowd swallows

my threadbare bear; kind hands bring
him home, still perfect.

By the time you reach the haiku, nearly all the details are gone—but the feeling remains. That's the point of ultra-short memoir: to give readers just enough to feel the weight of your memory while letting their imagination fill in the rest. Whether you stop at 50 words or push yourself into the strict limits of a haiku, the process forces you to decide what matters most.

Annotations: How the Story Shrinks Without Losing Its Heart, add as a side section to the above.

300 Words → 50 Words
What stayed:

- Core friend, search, reunion.
- Key emotional beats: loss, failed comfort, retrieval, joy.
- The "you can't fake history" line — keeps personality and theme plot (bear lost, parents' failed replacement attempt.

What went:

- Descriptive padding ("smelled faintly of grass and cookies," "seams stretched, button eyes loose") — these enrich the long version but aren't essential for the short form.
- Scene details of the search (under benches, between folding chairs) — cut for brevity.
- Comedic closing line about coffee — sacrificed to keep a focus on the bear.

50 Words → Single Sentence

What stayed:

- Emotional arc compressed into a single cause-and-effect: friend found lost bear → joy at reunion.
- Descriptors "faded, limp, and perfect" — imagery keeps emotional resonance.

What went:

- Parents' replacement attempt — extra subplot removed to keep line clean.
- Parade route detail — implied in "after the Easter parade."

Why:

- A single sentence can't hold multiple threads; focus on the reunion moment as the emotional climax.

Single Sentence → Haiku

What stayed:

- Core loss-and-return arc.
- Emotional tone (loss → kindness → restoration).
- Central image of the bear being "perfect" despite wear.

What went:

- Friend character — implied as "kind hands" without naming.
- Parade detail — reduced to "Easter crowd" to save syllables.

Why:

- Haiku's 17-syllable constraint forces imagery over narrative detail.

The Reduction Ladder

It's your turn to practice the art of saying more with less. Follow these steps to take one memory through the full reduction process—from a full scene to its most distilled form.

Step 1 – Write the Full Version (up to 300 words)

Tell the story in detail:

- Include the setting, characters, and what happened.
- Use sensory details (what you saw, heard, smelled, touched, tasted).
- Let the emotion come through naturally—don't rush to the end.

Step 2 – Cut to 50 Words

- Keep only the *core plot* and one or two vivid images.
- Remove side characters, extra dialogue, and nonessential descriptions.
- Ask: "If I only had 10 seconds to tell this story, what would I say?"

Step 3 – Reduce to a Single Sentence

- Focus on the *emotional climax* or *turning point*.
- Avoid multiple subplots—pick one thread and stick to it.

- Let implication carry the rest.

Step 4 – Write the Haiku

- 5–7–5 syllable structure.
- Capture one image or feeling from the story.
- Keep it concrete—show, don't tell.

Pro Tip: Read your haiku aloud. If it still stirs the same feeling as your full version, you've found the story's heartbeat.

Chapter 8

When to Go Longer — Letting Your Story Breathe

Some stories need more room to unfold. You can try to squeeze them into a micro-memoir, but you'll feel the loss—emotional beats will vanish, context will flatten, and nuance will evaporate. Longer forms allow you to honour the complexity of an experience, give space for reflection, and let characters grow in the reader's mind.

Signs Your Story Needs More Space

1. **Multiple Emotional Beats**

   If your memory contains more than one turning point—loss followed by reconciliation, shock followed by humour—it will likely need a longer arc to let each moment land.

2. **Complex Context**

   Historical, cultural, or relational backdrops can enrich your story, but they take space to explain. If your reader won't "get it" without context, don't starve the details.

3. **Layered Experiences**

   Some events carry more than one thread—trauma woven with personal growth, or tragedy braided with absurdity. These can be powerful in short form, but a longer piece lets the layers unfold without rushing.

Micro-Memoir vs. Short Essay

- Micro-Memoir: A single, self-contained moment or emotional core. Often 300 words or fewer.
- Short Essay: A wider arc—often a series of connected moments leading to a bigger reflection. Usually 1,000–3,000 words.

Pacing: Micro-memoirs are a single breath; short essays have a rhythm of inhale–pause–exhale.

Purpose: Micro-memoirs capture; essays explore.

Expanding Without Rambling

- The "Every Paragraph Earns Its Keep" Rule: Each paragraph must advance the story, deepen emotion, or add necessary context. If it doesn't, cut it.
- Vary the Zoom Lens: Move between close-up moments (sensory details, dialogue) and wide shots (context, reflection).
- Build with Intent: Ask yourself: "If I had one more page, what additional layer could I reveal?"

From Micro to Macro

One of the easiest ways to write a longer memoir piece is to take an existing 300-word micro-memoir and expand it into a 1,500–3,000 word essay. You already have the emotional core—now you can:

- Add backstory and context.
- Include more scenes and characters.
- Weave in reflection and thematic depth.

Example Expansion

Original Micro-Memoir (151 words):

At the Easter parade, my teddy vanished. My parents tried replacing him with a "well-loved" impostor, but you can't fake history. A family friend retraced the parade route, asking shopkeepers, "Anyone seen a teddy?" Hours later, he returned the faded, limp bear to my arms—perfect, just as he was.

Expanded Essay Opening (excerpt from a hypothetical 2,000-word version):

The Easter parade was a blur of brass horns and pastel hats, the kind of spring day that made the air smell like sugar. I was four, maybe five, and gripping my teddy with one hand and a melted marshmallow chick with the other. By then, Teddy was more thread than fluff, one ear held on by stubbornness and whatever magic keeps beloved things from falling apart. Somewhere between the fire truck and the high school marching band, he disappeared. It wasn't a dramatic gasp-and-drop—I simply turned my head, and he was gone. The world shifted.

That afternoon became a map of grief and hope: the toy store, the failed stand-in, the long search by a family friend, and the moment my arms folded around him again. In those few hours, I learned some losses are temporary—and some loves stay ragged and perfect forever.

When a Micro-Memoir Becomes the Seed of a Book

Pay attention to your own writing. If you notice:

- You keep returning to the same themes (loss, resilience, belonging).
- Your micro-memoir feels like a single tile in a much larger mosaic.
- Readers keep saying, "I want to hear more about that."

...then you may be sitting on a book idea.

First step: Outline a longer narrative arc. Identify the "big story" and see how your short pieces could be woven together, with connective chapters filling in the spaces between.

Expansion Drill

1. Choose one of your micro-memoirs (150–300 words).

2. List three questions your reader might still have after reading it.
3. Answer those questions in full paragraphs—this is your starting expansion.
4. Add context, reflection, and additional scenes until you reach at least 1,500 words.

Playing with Scale for Maximum Impact

When you're building a collection of memoirs, variety in length can be just as important as variety in tone. Imagine reading page after page of 300-word pieces—each lovely in its own right, but eventually blending together in rhythm. Now imagine a book where a single-sentence story follows a 2,000-word essay, which is then followed by a 50-word vignette and a haiku. The shifts in scale create surprise, breathing room, and momentum.

Ultra-short pieces act like quick flashes—emotional snapshots that give the reader a moment of intensity before letting them move on. Longer essays invite them to settle in, absorb layers, and live with the story for a while. Together, these forms create a natural ebb and flow, much like conversation, where brief remarks and deep talks mingle.

By mastering both ends of the spectrum, you can shape a collection that keeps readers engaged not only in your stories but in *how* you tell them. Variety of length is more than a stylistic choice—it's a structural tool for intrigue, pacing, and resonance.

Chapter 9

Writing in Stereo—The Power of Dual Perspective

Sharing the Burden

Writing a memoir can feel heavy when you carry it alone. With a partner—a sibling, a spouse, a friend—you share the emotional load. Where one voice falters, the other fills in. This partnership can make it easier to tackle tough stories or simply make the process more fun.

Doubling the Creativity

Two minds bring double the images, quirks, and memories. One person might remember the smell of the campfire, while the other recalls the way the smoke stung their eyes. Combined, the story feels richer, layered, and true in multiple dimensions.

Taking Different Perspectives

A single event is rarely experienced the same way by two people. A dual memoir can highlight:

- Contrasts: Fear vs. excitement, humour vs. tension.
- Blind spots: What you missed, someone else might have seen.
- Evolution: How the same memory changes when viewed through different eyes.

Micro-Memoir - Shared Arrival, Dual Perspective

Mother: Exhaustion blurred everything—the white walls, the nurse's voice, even the tiny bundle in my arms. And yet, when I looked down, I felt a love so fierce it frightened me. For months, this child had been mine alone, sheltered inside me. Now, in a rush of light and air, she belonged to the world. To grandparents, to strangers who would one day teach her, to friends I hadn't even met yet. She was no longer only mine, and I felt the ache of letting go even as I kissed her damp forehead.

Father: I stood beside the bed, useless hands gripping the rail. I had watched her pain and could do nothing. Now I stared at this red-faced, wailing child and thought: *How can I possibly be enough?* I am no healer, no protector of great strength. My wife has already proven herself—she brought life into being. And me? I can only stand guard, hoping my presence matters, hoping one day this child will see me as more than a witness.

Mother: I closed my eyes, heavy with sleep. The world outside could wait. For now, she was still pressed against me, still my secret.

Father: I reached for her tiny fist. It closed around my finger. In that grip, I felt my answer: I didn't need to be everything. I just needed to stay.
Word Count: 228

Annotation: Micro-Memoir-Shared Arrival, Dual Perspective

- Dual Voice: Alternating "Mother" and "Father" sections highlight contrast—love vs. fear, surrender vs. inadequacy.
- Shared Theme: Both arcs wrestle with *identity shift*: she from "mine" to "ours," he from "outsider" to "present father."
- Intimacy through Detail: Simple images—kissing a damp forehead, a fist closing around a finger—carry emotional weight without over-explaining.
- Resolution: Father's closing realization balances the mother's earlier ache, leaving the story unified in hope.

Braided Micro-Memoir: Grand Opening

Alex:
I woke before dawn, palms sweaty, imagining empty chairs. What if no one showed?

Jordan:
I was already at the shop, arranging pastries like soldiers on a battlefield. If the coffee didn't sell, at least the muffins would.

Alex:
We taped the "Grand Opening" sign to the window. The tape peeled away once, twice, like it doubted us too.

Jordan:
But then the door jingled—our first customer. I nearly hugged them before they placed their order.

Alex:
The till stuck, my hand shook, but I counted the change, anyway.

Jordan:
I watched Alex laugh with a stranger and thought, 'We're really doing this.'

Alex:
The morning blurred into a haze of chatter and crumbs on tabletops.

Jordan:
When we finally locked the door, exhausted, the air smelled of coffee grounds and victory.

Both:
We had built something together. And people had come.
Word Count: 166

Annotation: Braided Micro-Memoir – Grand Opening

- Identifiers: Using names at the start of each fragment ensures clarity while keeping the braid tight.
- Alternation: Each perspective bounces off the other—Alex's nerves countered by Jordan's pragmatism, then reversed.
- Concrete detail: Pastries as "soldiers," tape peeling, till sticking—ground the story in sensory reality.
- Shared resolution: Ends with both voices unified, giving the story closure and highlighting partnership.

Digging Deep with an Interview

One effective method is to use a Q&A approach:

- Person A writes about the event.
- Person B responds with questions, clarifications, or challenges.

- Together, they uncover hidden layers—sometimes uncomfortable truths.

This pressure often sharpens the story, forcing each writer to defend or expand their version.

Alternatively, the interview method works well with children who cannot document their own memoir, but the perspective is often entertaining.

Micro-Memoir: New Skies

Parent: What did you think of the airplane?
Child: It was loud. Like a dragon who forgot to whisper.

Parent: Were you scared?
Child: No, my belly tickled when it went up. Like a swing, but higher.

Parent: What about the clouds?
Child: They're not soft. They're just outside the window. I wanted to touch them, but the glass said no.

Parent: And now—what do you see here?

Child: The ground smells different. The trees don't look like home. But the sky followed us!

Parent: Do you like it?
Child: Yes… but where are Grandma's hugs?

The parent scribbled the answers down that evening, realizing the child's words carried both wonder and a hint of homesickness. It was their first flight, their first country beyond their own—and already, the child understood what stayed the same and what had changed.

Word Count: 131

Adding Productive Pressure

Sometimes, two voices create tension on the page. That tension can be productive. Maybe one insists, *"You always exaggerate."* The other counters, *"But that's how it felt to me."* The friction sparks energy, making the memoir feel alive and real.

Formats to Try

- **He Said / She Said:** Alternating short sections like a conversation.
- **Braided Narrative:** Two parallel accounts that weave together at key points.
- **Annotated Memory:** One writer narrates, the other adds side comments, corrections, or reflections in the margins.

Dual Point-of-View

Choose one memory you share with someone else. Write your version in 150 words. Then invite them to write theirs—without reading yours first. Put the two side by side. What overlaps? What surprises you? What contradictions emerge? That's the beauty of memory in stereo.

Chapter 10

Artifacts as Memoirs

Preserving Life in Its Original Packaging

Not all memoir writing starts with a blank page. Sometimes the most powerful pieces come from things you've already written—or that someone has written to you. These fragments of life, what I call *artifacts*, can be postcards, letters, greeting cards, ticket stubs, emails, text messages, voicemails, grocery lists—anything that captures a genuine moment in time.

Artifacts carry a special kind of truth because they're unfiltered. They were not crafted for an audience or polished for publication. They are time capsules—keeping the voice, mood, and even the quirks of grammar and spelling intact. When included in a memoir, they can instantly transport readers back to a moment with startling intimacy.

Why Artifacts Work

Artifacts shift the rhythm of a memoir collection. In a sea of well-crafted prose, a raw postcard or one-line grocery list can feel like an unplanned glimpse behind the curtain. They:

- Change pacing by providing short, powerful pauses between longer narratives.
- Deepen authenticity because they're unedited snapshots of real interactions.
- Preserve voices—sometimes literally, in the case of voicemails or recordings.
- Invite emotion through brevity—a few words can feel heavier than pages of description.

Types of Artifacts You Might Use

- Postcards & Letters: Travel updates, love notes, confessions.
- Emails & Texts: Modern equivalents of letters, often capturing in-the-moment tone.
- Lists: Grocery, to-do, bucket lists; their contents can be surprisingly revealing.
- Voicemails & Phone Messages: The voice of someone who may no longer be here.
- Cards & Invitations: Birthdays, weddings, graduations, even events you didn't attend.
- Receipts & Tickets: Proof of a shared experience or a turning point in life.

Fictionalised Examples

1. The Postcard from Paris

Postcard text:

"They still serve croissants as big as your head at that café by the river. I miss you more than butter misses bread."

Reflection: I was nineteen, working double shifts, and the closest I got to Paris that year was the Eiffel Tower keychain my friend tucked in the envelope with this postcard. It still smells faintly of her perfume.

2. The Unsent Love Letter

Letter text (excerpt):

"I'm writing this because I can't seem to say it out loud: you've changed my life in ways you'll never understand. I don't know if this is love, but I know it's something I want to keep."

Reflection: I found this in a box labelled "college stuff" when I moved last spring. The letter was dated three weeks before we broke up. He never gave it to me.

3. The Voicemail

Transcript: *"Hey, it's me. I just made your favourite soup. Call me when you're on your way home, and I'll heat it up."*

Reflection: That was my mother's voice. She left the message five days before she died. The voicemail box is full now, but I'll never delete that one.

4. The Grocery List

List:

- Milk
- Bread
- Bananas
- Don't forget the good coffee!

Reflection: It's the exclamation point that gets me. He always took coffee seriously, even when everything else in our marriage was falling apart.

How to Present an Artifact

1. As-Is: Let it stand alone without commentary for maximum impact.
2. With a Reflection: Follow the artifact with a brief personal note that gives context or emotional depth.
3. With Visual Reproduction: Include a scan or photo of the original for a tactile sense of the moment.

When the Artifact Is Gone

Sometimes, the tangible pieces of our past get lost—boxes left behind in a move, water damage in a basement, or a deleted voicemail you swore you'd never erase. That doesn't mean the story is gone. In a memoir, absence can be just as powerful as presence. You can recreate an artifact from memory and still present it authentically, as long as you're clear with your reader.

Be Transparent

If the original is missing, label the piece as *recreated from memory* or *based on recollection*. A simple note tells the reader you've done your best to stay true without pretending it's exact.

Example Title: *Postcard from Rome (Recreated from Memory)*

Capture the Spirit, Not Just the Words

When you can't remember the exact phrasing, focus on:

- Tone: Was it teasing, loving, formal, or rushed?
- Quirks: Misspellings, inside jokes, pet names.
- Emotional residue: How you felt when you first read or heard it.

Use Fragments Honestly

If you only recall parts, present them as fragments rather than trying to fill in every blank.

Example: *I don't remember the whole voicemail, but I remember she said: "It's a blue-sky day—don't waste it indoors." I can still hear her laugh after she said it.*

Make the Absence Part of the Story

Sometimes, losing the artifact adds another layer of meaning. The void itself can be a narrative thread.

Example: *The postcard is gone—probably tossed during my last move. But I remember the handwriting: looping, impatient, the ink smudged where she'd dropped it in her coffee. I think I miss the smudge most of all.*

By acknowledging what's missing, you're still honouring the truth of your experience. A recreated artifact can be just as moving as the original—sometimes even more so, because it's infused with the haze and tenderness of memory.

Mining Your Life for Artifacts

Artifacts don't live in your imagination—they live in your drawers, boxes, and digital archives. Let's find some.

Step 1 – Hunt for Keepsakes

- Dig into old boxes, storage bins, or folders on your phone/computer.
- Look for: postcards, greeting cards, notes, letters, emails, printed receipts, ticket stubs, scribbled lists, voicemails, or texts.

Step 2 – Choose One That Speaks

- Pick an artifact that makes you feel *something*—joy, grief, nostalgia, longing, even irritation.
- Make sure it represents a specific person, moment, or relationship.

Step 3 – Decide How to Present It

- Will you show it as-is?

- Or will you follow it with a short reflection that gives context and emotional weight?

Step 4 – Give It a Title

- Titles act as tiny frames around your artifact—choose one that hints at the story or emotion behind it.

Pro Tip: If you include multiple artifacts in your collection, vary the type and tone—mix a playful postcard with a gut-punch voicemail, a love letter with a terse email. The variety will keep your reader turning pages.

Part III

From Memory to Manuscript

Chapter 11

Memory Mining Techniques

Every memoir, whether micro-short or sprawling, begins with memory. But memory is slippery—it hides, it fades, it rearranges itself when we're not looking. To build a rich body of material, you need to go beyond waiting for stories to "come to you." Memory mining is about actively searching your mental archives, coaxing moments out of hiding, and giving them a place to land.

The good news? You already have the raw material. You just need to know where to dig.

Sensory Prompts: Awakening Dormant Memories

Our senses are wired directly to the brain's emotional core. A smell, sound, or texture can crack open a door to the past that you didn't even know was closed.

- Smell: The scent of chlorine might bring back summers at the community pool.

- Sound: The distant clatter of dishes could remind you of a childhood kitchen.
- Touch: The scratch of wool might conjure the sweater your grandmother knit.
- Taste: One bite of a certain bread might return you instantly to a street market abroad.

Try this: Close your eyes, pick a sense, and free-write for five minutes about the first memory that surfaces—don't edit, just capture.

Memory Maps: Plotting the Past

Sometimes memories return more easily when you give them a visual frame. A *memory map* is a rough sketch of a location from your past—a house, a school, a favourite street. As you draw, label each room or corner with the strongest memory attached to it.

Example: Drawing your childhood bedroom might remind you of the poster that fell during a storm, the creaky spot in the floor you avoided at night, or the secret stash of candy in the desk drawer. Each detail can be the seed for a micro-memoir.

Object Triggers: The Tangible Story-Starters

Objects are excellent portals into memory because they carry the fingerprints of our lives.

- A watch that stopped working the day your grandfather died.

- The coffee mug from your first apartment.
- A folded note you carried in your wallet for years.

Pro Tip: Walk through your home with a small notebook and jot down objects that feel heavy with meaning. You'll be surprised at how quickly the list grows.

Using Journaling as Source Material

If you keep a journal, you already have a treasure chest of potential memoir content. The act of journaling is therapeutic because it bypasses the inner editor—when we write for ourselves, we tend to be raw, unfiltered, and emotionally honest.

When mining journals for memoir:

- Look for recurring themes or phrases.
- Notice entries that still make you feel something as you read them.
- Don't be afraid to reframe an old journal entry into a new piece—time can change your perspective and deepen the story.

Mining Oral History: The Stories That Live in the Air

Not every story in your memoir has to come from your direct experience. Families, friend groups, and communities have *shared stories*—tales told so often they become part of the collective memory. These are the stories that come up at every family gathering, that your children can recite even though they weren't there, that feel just as vivid as your own memories.

Sometimes, they're moments of triumph, sometimes embarrassment, and sometimes just everyday mishaps elevated to legend.

There's the story of my sister, who put a pot of water on the stove for macaroni...and fell asleep. The smell of burning metal woke her later, the water long gone, the pot scorched. She did it again two more times over the next few months until she was banned from boiling water. This story gets told so often that even my children—born decades later—can tell it beat for beat, embellishing it with the exact pauses and laughter they've heard at the dinner table for years.

When you include these kinds of stories in a memoir, you're capturing more than an event—you're preserving a shared cultural artifact. You are demonstrating how stories evolve over time, shaped by each retelling.

How to capture oral history in your memoir:

- Write the version you've heard most often, in the voice you've heard it told.
- Make note of the *ritual* of the telling—when, where, and who brings it up.
- Include variations. Do different family members tell it differently?
- Decide whether to keep the "family myth" intact or clarify what's fact and what's fiction.

Oral history is a reminder that memoir isn't just about what *you* remember—it's also about the stories you've inherited. They might not be *your* memories, but they live in you just the same.

Memory mining isn't about forcing your brain to cough up perfectly packaged stories. It's about gathering raw material—snapshots, fragments, impressions—that you can shape later. You may not use every memory you uncover, but the act of collecting them builds a foundation of richness and authenticity for your memoir.

Now Your Turn

Your First Memory Harvest

This exercise will guide you through multiple memory-mining techniques, so by the end, you'll have a starting bank of at least 10–15 story seeds.

Step 1 – Sensory Sparks

- Choose **one sense** (smell, sound, touch, taste, sight).
- Close your eyes and recall a vivid memory linked to that sense.
- Write for 5 minutes without stopping—don't edit.
- Repeat with a different sense tomorrow for more variety.

Step 2 – Map Your Memory Spaces

- Draw a quick map of an important place from your past (childhood home, school, summer camp, workplace).

- Label rooms or areas with events, people, or feelings tied to them.
- Pick one label and free-write for 10 minutes.

Step 3 – Object Hunt

- Walk through your home and note objects that trigger emotion or curiosity.
- Write 1–2 lines about the story behind each.
- Star the ones that make you smile, wince, or tear up—those are prime memoir seeds.

Step 4 – Journal Dive

- If you keep journals, flip through and mark entries that still stir emotion.
- Summarize each in one or two sentences.
- For older entries, note how your perspective has changed since you wrote them.

Step 5 – Capture Oral History

- List the stories told repeatedly at family gatherings or among friends.
- Choose one and write it as you've heard it told—include quirks, catchphrases, and who usually tells it.
- Optional: Add a short note about how hearing it has shaped your sense of family or identity.

Step 6 – Reflect & Sort

- Look over everything you've written from steps 1–5.

- Circle the top 3 memories you most want to expand into micro-memoirs.
- Keep the rest in a “memory bank” for future writing sessions.

Chapter 12

Overcoming Writer's Block

Why the Blank Page Feels So Heavy?

Writer's block isn't a sign you're "not a real writer." It's often the opposite—it means you care about what you're trying to say. But caring too much can put your creativity in a chokehold. Whether your block shows up as procrastination, endless tinkering, or the inability to start, the key is to lower the stakes and get words flowing again.

Creative Warm-Ups

Just like athletes stretch before a game, writers can "stretch" their creative muscles to loosen up. These warm-ups are quick, low-pressure, and often silly—perfect for tricking your brain into motion.

- Random Word Sprint: Pick a word at random from a book or online generator and write a 5-sentence memory that includes it.

- Memory Chain: Start with a single memory, then let it trigger another, and another, until you have a list of 10. Pick one to explore further.
- Sensory Blast: Describe what you can see, hear, and smell right where you're sitting. Even mundane details can turn into story material.

The goal here is not perfection—it's movement.

The "One Sitting" Method

Some pieces become easier to write when you commit to finishing them in one go, without editing. This method works best for micro-memoirs, flash nonfiction, and emotional snapshots.

How it works:

1. Set a timer for 20–30 minutes.
2. Choose a specific, contained memory (no sprawling life arcs).
3. Write from start to finish without stopping to reread or correct.

When the timer dings, you have a complete draft. It may be messy, but it exists—which is already a victory. Editing can happen later.

Breaking Down Resistance into Tiny Steps

Sometimes writer's block comes from asking too much of yourself in one sitting. Instead of "write a chapter," try breaking the task into small, non-threatening actions:

- Open your notebook.
- Write one sentence.
- Write for 5 minutes, no more.
- Describe an object from your memory bank.

These micro-tasks lower the activation energy required to initiate the process. Often once you've started, momentum builds naturally.

The secret to overcoming writer's block isn't brute force—it's gentleness. By shifting the focus from "writing something great" to "writing something at all," you give yourself permission to bypass fear and perfectionism.

One Week to Break the Block

This 7-day plan combines creative warm-ups, the One Sitting method, and tiny-step resistance breakers. The aim isn't to produce polished memoirs—it's to rebuild your writing momentum.

Day 1 – Random Spark

- Open a book at random, point to a word, and write a 5-sentence memory using it.
- Don't worry about logic—just connect the dots however you can.

Day 2 – Memory Chain

- Start with one vivid memory. Let it trigger another, and another, until you have a list of 10.

- Pick the most surprising one and jot down 3 quick details.

Day 3 – The One Sitting Micro-Memoir

- Set a timer for 25 minutes.
- Choose a single moment you can describe fully in that time.
- Write start to finish, no stopping, no editing.

Day 4 – Sensory Dive

- Sit somewhere familiar. Spend 5 minutes noting everything you can see, hear, and smell.
- Circle one detail that feels like the start of a story and write a paragraph about it.

Day 5 – Object Story

- Choose an item from your memory bank.
- Write about its history in 150 words or fewer.

Day 6 – Ultra-Tiny Step

1. Write one sentence about your day.
2. Then, if you feel like it, write a second. No pressure—if one is all you do, you've still succeeded.

Day 7 – Stretch & Reflect

- Pick your favourite piece from the week and expand it for 15 minutes.
- Note which exercises felt easiest and which uncovered the best material.

Pro Tip: Repeat this plan any time you hit a block. Over time, you'll learn which quick-start techniques work best for you—and your "restart" will get faster.

Chapter 13

Editing for Impact

Why Editing Matters Just as Much as Writing

When you first put words on paper, you're capturing the raw energy of your story. Editing is where you turn that energy into something sharp, clear, and powerful. Think of it like sculpting—you start with a full block of marble, but the magic happens as you chip away everything that doesn't belong.

Editing for memoirs—especially micro-memoirs—isn't about trimming to fit a word count. It's about making sure every single word carries its weight, so the final piece feels inevitable, like it couldn't have been written any other way.

Cutting Without Losing the Heart

The most difficult part of editing is letting go of words you love. But the heart of your story doesn't live in its length—it lives in its essence.

How to protect the heart while cutting:

- Identify the emotional core: What is this story *really* about? Everything else should serve that.
- Remove redundancy: If you've said it once well, you don't need to say it again.
- Test with "so what?": After each sentence, ask yourself: If I cut this, does the story lose meaning?

Example:

Original: *The rain poured down hard, soaking us through to the skin, dripping from our noses and eyelashes.*

Edited: *The rain soaked us to the skin.*→ The image is still vivid, but the sentence moves faster. Both are good sentences; edit only what you want.

Making Every Word Earn Its Place

In a memoir, every word must carry story, tone, or emotion—or its excess baggage.

Quick checks:

- Does this word add precision or just padding?
- Can I use one stronger word instead of three weaker ones?
- Is this adjective doing real work, or is it just sitting there?

Tools for Finding Stronger Words

Sometimes, the best edit isn't cutting—it's swapping a bland word for one that sings.

- Thesaurus: Use with caution; you're not hunting for fancy words, you're looking for *truer* ones. The word that resonates with the tone and sentiment.
- Language Cross-Pollination: If you speak more than one language, consider words from your other tongues. Sometimes there's no direct translation for the feeling you mean, and borrowing that word adds richness. (*Saudade,* Portuguese, meaning a deep, nostalgic longing, can express something English can't capture in one word.)
- Contextual Replacement: Instead of "walked quickly," use "hurried," "strode," or "rushed"—each carries a different nuance.

Editing doesn't make your story sterile—it makes it inevitable. It ensures that nothing distracts from the emotion you're trying to deliver, and that each word is placed with intention.

Part IV

The Purpose & Reach of Your Micro-Memoir

Chapter 14

Micro-Memoirs That Change Minds

Every single person carries a lens through which they see the world—and that lens colours how they tell their story. This perspective may be shaped by your culture, but it can also stem from your work, hobbies, or life experiences.

A firefighter might notice evacuation routes in a restaurant before the menu. A teacher might find themselves explaining a concept in real life as if the listener were a classroom of twenty-five. A veterinarian might remember an entire event through the smell of antiseptic and the sound of an anxious pet.

You don't need a uniform or a title for your perspective to matter. The lens of "you today" can be wildly different from the lens of "you back then"—even if the only difference is time. Writing a micro-memoir is a kind of mini-therapy session with your past self, where you hold a moment in your hands, turn it in the light, and see what you notice now that you couldn't see then.

Short Stories, Big Shifts

Micro-memoirs are small in size but have a powerful impact. A well-crafted 200-word story about one injustice you witnessed—or one kindness you received—can lodge in a reader's mind more deeply than a full-length speech.

You don't have to set out to "inspire social change" for it to happen. Change often comes from the emotional truth of your personal experience, not from an agenda. Readers connect with a real human moment, and then they carry that connection into how they see the world.

Weaving in Cultural Heritage

Cultural perspective in memoir is more than just where your family came from—it's the language you use, the foods you remember, the holidays you celebrated or ignored, the rules you thought were universal but weren't.

These details can add texture to your story even if the theme isn't directly about culture. For example:

- A story about learning to drive could also include the fact that you learned in your grandfather's farm truck, with his old country radio playing in the background.
- A memory about grief could weave in a cultural mourning ritual, showing how your community expresses loss. Or in my case, how the cultural expectations did not align with how my mind wanted to grieve.

Even if you're writing from a dominant culture or background, your perspective is still unique—it's shaped by the family, neighbourhood, and social environment that raised you.

The Past You vs. The Present You

One of the most striking ways to use perspective is to revisit a memory from the viewpoint of who you are now. This dual lens creates a layered narrative: the raw immediacy of the moment, and the reflective wisdom (or humour, or regret) of hindsight.

For example:

- Past you: "I thought if I aced the interview, I'd get the job."
- Present you: "Now I know the interview was the easy part; the real test was surviving my first month."

This contrast can make even a short memoir feel emotionally rich.

Seeing the Same Memory Twice

One of the simplest yet most revealing techniques in memoir writing is to tell the same moment from two different vantage points—the "you" who lived it and the "you" who reflects on it now. This past–present contrast works because it layers raw, unfiltered experience with the wisdom, humour, or even disillusionment that time brings. In the example below, the same summer trip to Kawartha Dairy is told first through the wide-eyed lens of a child, then through the wry, detail-rich lens of an adult. Neither version is more "true" than the other—they simply highlight how perspective reshapes memory.

Two Lenses, One Memory – Kawartha Dairy

Child Lens:

It was the hottest day of the summer, the kind where the air feels like warm syrup and your shadow bakes on the pavement. The whole family—so many people we needed more than one car—piled in to drive to Kawartha Dairy. I could already taste the bubble gum ice cream I was going to choose, those pink and blue swirls that made my tongue change colour. While the parents got our cones, we tumbled down the giant hill outside, grass stains decorating our knees. The picnic table was warm against my bare legs, but I didn't care—the ice cream was cold, perfect, and dripping in my hand. I thought there could never be another moment this good.

Word Count: 120

Child lens is pure immediacy—size, taste, and joy are exaggerated because that's how memory works when you're small.

Adult Lens:

Looking back now, I know it wasn't "the whole family." It was five kids and two tired mothers who needed to get us out of the house before we staged a mutiny. The "giant hill" was really a four-foot grassy slope beside the parking lot. The bubble gum ice cream was sweeter than my teeth could

stand, melting faster than I could keep up. My mom kept grabbing it to reshape the cone, muttering about how awful it tasted. And then my sister's scoop plopped to the ground, tears immediately following—until she got a brand-new cone. To this day, I wonder if she dropped it on purpose.
Word Count: 108

Adult lens provides perspective, humour, and gentle skepticism, reshaping the memory without erasing the original magic.

Two Lenses, One Memory (Fictionalized) – The Winter Concert

Child Lens:

The gym was packed, and I was sure every single person in the town had come to see me sing. My brand-new red dress sparkled under the stage lights, and I gripped the songbook like a treasure. Mom sat in the front row, waving so big I thought her hand might fly right off. When it was my turn to sing my solo, I took a deep breath and let the words float up to the ceiling. The applause felt like fireworks. That night, I went to sleep thinking I might grow up to be famous.
Word Count: 96

Child lens captures the inflated scale of childhood memory, turning a small-town concert into a world stage.

Adult Lens:

I know now the gym wasn't "packed"—there were maybe 50 people in metal folding chairs, most of them parents who had rushed straight from work. The red dress had been on clearance, and the hem was held up by safety pins. My solo was only four lines long, and my voice cracked on the third. Mom's wave was bigger than I remembered, probably to distract me from looking so nervous. I see now it wasn't a crowd I was singing for—it was her. And she made sure I felt like the whole room was mine.

Word Count: 97

Adult lens reframes the scene with grounded detail and emotional truth, revealing the love and effort behind the moment.

Two Lenses, One Story

Choose one vivid memory—big or small—that has stayed with you. It could be from your early childhood, teen years, or even just a few years ago. Then, write it twice:

1. **Past Lens** – Write it exactly as you experienced it in the moment.
   - Use sensory details the way you remember them.
   - Allow for exaggeration, confusion, or incomplete understanding—your past self didn't have all the context.
   - Keep the voice and perspective true to the "you" from that time.
2. **Present Lens** – Revisit the same memory as the person you are now.

- Add context you didn't know at the time.
- Include new interpretations, humour, or even gentle corrections to your earlier version.
- Show how the meaning or scale of the event has shifted.

Tips to get started:

- Pick a moment that sparks emotion—even a small one like a family picnic, a school project, or your first solo bus ride.
- Pay attention to how your tone changes between the two versions.
- Don't erase the child or past self's version—let it live alongside your current perspective.

Challenge: Share both versions with a friend or writing group and ask which parts resonated most with them. You may find that the combination, rather than either version alone, has the greatest impact.

Chapter 15

Preserving and Sharing Your Work

Not every micro-memoir is meant for a bookstore shelf. Some are treasures you'll want to keep within your family, share only with close friends, or preserve as a private record for future generations. Just because a piece isn't public doesn't mean it's any less important. In fact, private memoirs often carry a deeper intimacy, because you're free to write without the pressure of a wide audience.

Creating a Personal Archive

Your micro-memoirs deserve a safe home. A personal archive can be as simple as a shoebox or as elaborate as a bound, illustrated book.

Options include:

- Physical Notebooks or Binders: Keep printed copies of your stories, photos, or mementos alongside them.

- Digital Folders: Create dated folders on your computer or cloud storage so everything is easy to search later.
- Specialty Keepsake Books: Print-on-demand services let you turn your collection into a beautiful hardcover for family use only.
- Audio or Video Recordings: If your voice or expressions are part of the story's charm, consider reading your micro-memoirs aloud and recording them.
- Blog post, digital newsletter, or social media platforms.

Pro Tip: Use clear file names and dates, especially for digital archives. Your future self—and your descendants—will thank you.

Sharing Online in a Private Way

You don't have to post your writing publicly to share it digitally. Consider:

- Private Facebook Groups: Invite only family and close friends.
- Google Drive or Dropbox Links: Share with specific people via email invitations.
- Private Blogs or Newsletters: Platforms like Substack or WordPress allow password-protected content.
- Messaging Apps: Send micro-memoirs as part of a family group chat on WhatsApp, Messenger, or Signal.

Even in private spaces, digital content can be screenshot or forwarded. Share only what you're comfortable leaving your circle.

Turning Micro-Memoirs into Family Keepsakes

Writing a family history doesn't have to mean a 300-page genealogical tome. It can be a collection of micro-memoirs woven together into a scrapbook-style document.

- Include photos, recipes, and scanned letters alongside your stories.
- Group pieces by theme: Holidays, School Days, Family Pets…
- Add captions and dates so future readers understand the context.

Example: One family printed their grandmother's micro-memoirs as a small zine for Christmas. Each grandchild got a copy filled with short stories about her childhood, her marriage, and funny parenting moments. Tucked into the back pocket was a photocopy of her favourite handwritten recipe card.

The Gift of Legacy

When you share your writing privately, you're giving your family something no one else can—a record of their people in their own voices. Years from now, someone might find your micro-memoir about a summer trip or a kitchen mishap and suddenly feel connected to you in a way a formal biography never could.

Your stories don't have to be loud to be lasting. They just have to be told.

Ethical Dilemmas of Revealing Family Secrets (Navigating Truth and Fiction)

One of the hardest parts of memoir writing is that your story often overlaps with someone else's. What you write may expose private information about family, friends, or colleagues—whether or not you intend it to.

Questions to ask yourself before revealing a shared story:

- Does this story belong solely to me, or does it deeply involve someone else?
- Have I considered how the other person might feel reading this?
- Am I prepared for the possibility of conflict, strained relationships, or even legal repercussions?

Strategies for protecting privacy:

- Change names, locations, and identifying details.
- Merge two or more real people into a single composite character.
- Use broad timeframes rather than exact dates if it's not crucial to the plot.
- When in doubt, ask for consent—especially if the person is still alive and identifiable.

A Note on Legal Liability

If you intend to publish your memoir publicly—whether through traditional publishing, self-publishing, or even posting it online—consider consulting a publishing lawyer, especially if your writing contains:

- Potentially defamatory statements about identifiable people.
- Sensitive or confidential information (medical records, financial details, criminal allegations).
- Stories that involve minors, criminal activity, or workplace incidents.

A publishing lawyer can help you:

- Assess the legal risk of specific passages.
- Suggest edits or anonymization to protect yourself.
- Navigate contracts and copyright issues.

It may feel like overkill for a short personal piece, but protecting yourself legally allows you to write with more confidence and fewer regrets later.

Legal Safety

- ☐ Does the piece contain statements that could be considered defamatory about identifiable people?
- ☐ Does it disclose sensitive information such as medical, financial, or legal matters about others?
- ☐ Does it include stories about minors, criminal activity, or workplace incidents?

- ☐ Have I considered consulting a publishing lawyer for legal review before release?
- ☐ If I'm using photos, quotes, or letters from others, do I have permission?

If you check *yes* to any of the legal risk items—or even if you're unsure—pause before publishing. A quick consultation with a publishing lawyer can prevent far bigger headaches later.

Your Private Legacy

1. **Choose Your Archive Style**
    - Will you keep your micro-memoirs in a physical format (notebook, binder, scrapbook) or digital format (folders, cloud storage, private blog)?
    - If you want both, decide how the two will work together—maybe digital drafts that you print annually into a keepsake book.
2. **Select 3–5 Micro-Memoirs to Start Your Collection**
    - Pick pieces that feel personal and timeless—stories you'd want future generations to know.
    - If they're currently handwritten or scattered across devices, gather them in one place.
3. **Decide Your Sharing Method**
    - **Private, In-Person:** Print and give only to chosen recipients (a family holiday gift, a birthday surprise).

- **Private, Digital:** Share via password-protected blog, private social media group, or direct file sharing.
- **Hybrid:** Create a physical book for keepsakes but also send digital copies for convenience.

4. **Add Personal Touches**

    - Pair each story with a photo, scan of a letter, or related artifact.
    - Write a short note introducing each piece—why you wrote it, or what it means to you.

5. **Mark the Date**

    - Include the year of creation or the time period the story covers.
    - This turns your collection into a chronological record of personal history.

Optional Challenge: Write a brief "Letter to the Future" to include with your micro-memoir collection, telling future readers what you hope they'll take from your stories.

Chapter 16

Publishing & Promotion

Not every collection of micro-memoirs belongs in a bookstore—but some absolutely do. You might want to publish because you believe your perspective could help someone navigate grief, inspire cultural understanding, or shed light on a career that rarely gets an insider's voice. A compilation of short pieces can be just as powerful as a single, sweeping memoir if it's built with an intentional narrative arc.

Your book doesn't have to cover your whole life—just a meaningful slice of it. Maybe it's a collection about your years as a new immigrant navigating a foreign country, or stories from your work as a first responder during the height of COVID-19. A focused theme, paired with your unique voice, gives your work purpose and makes it easier to connect with readers.

Self-Publishing Basics

For deeply personal or niche projects, self-publishing is often the best fit. You maintain control over:

- Content: No need to change your tone or cut stories that matter to you.
- Design: Choose layouts, fonts, and cover art that reflect your style.
- Distribution: Sell online, at events, or directly to your intended audience.

Steps to Self-Publish:

1. Edit & Proofread: Consider hiring a professional editor to ensure quality.
2. Format for Print & E-Book: Use platforms like Amazon Kindle Direct Publishing, IngramSpark, or BookBaby.
3. Choose Your Trim Size & Paper: Memoir compilations often work well in 5x8 or 6x9 sizes.
4. Upload & Approve Proofs: Always review a physical proof copy before going live.

Marketing Strategies That Actually Work

You don't need a massive budget to find your audience, but you need intention.

- Leverage Your Existing Network: Tell friends, family, and colleagues. Early support boosts visibility.
- Find Your Reader Communities: Join groups related to your theme (immigration support networks, career-specific forums, cultural associations).
- Use Social Media Selectively: Share excerpts, behind-the-scenes writing moments, or relevant commentary.

- Give Readings & Talks: Libraries, book clubs, and community centres often welcome local authors.
- Pitch Articles: Write essays or op-eds that connect to your book's theme to draw interest.

Leveraging Social Media for Micro-Memoirs

Micro-memoirs are uniquely suited to the short, high-impact nature of platforms like Instagram, Facebook, TikTok, and Twitter/X. A 100–200-word piece, paired with a striking image or video, can connect with readers in seconds and be shared widely.

Ways to use social media effectively:

- Share complete micro-memoirs: A short story can fit neatly into a caption or post, making it instantly accessible.
- Use visuals to amplify emotion: Pair text with photos, illustrations, or simple graphics to make the story scroll-stopping. There are free resources, such as Canva, that can help create stunning visuals.
- Create a series or themes: Posting in weekly or monthly batches helps readers follow along and anticipate your next piece.
- Engage with your audience: Invite readers to comment with their own experiences, turning your memoir into a conversation.
- Repurpose content: A micro-memoir can live in multiple formats—tweet-length lines, Instagram carousel slides, or short video narrations.

Pro Tip: Social media can also act as a "testing ground." By sharing pieces online, you can gauge which stories resonate most before finalizing your book manuscript.

Example: Instagram Micro-Memoir Post

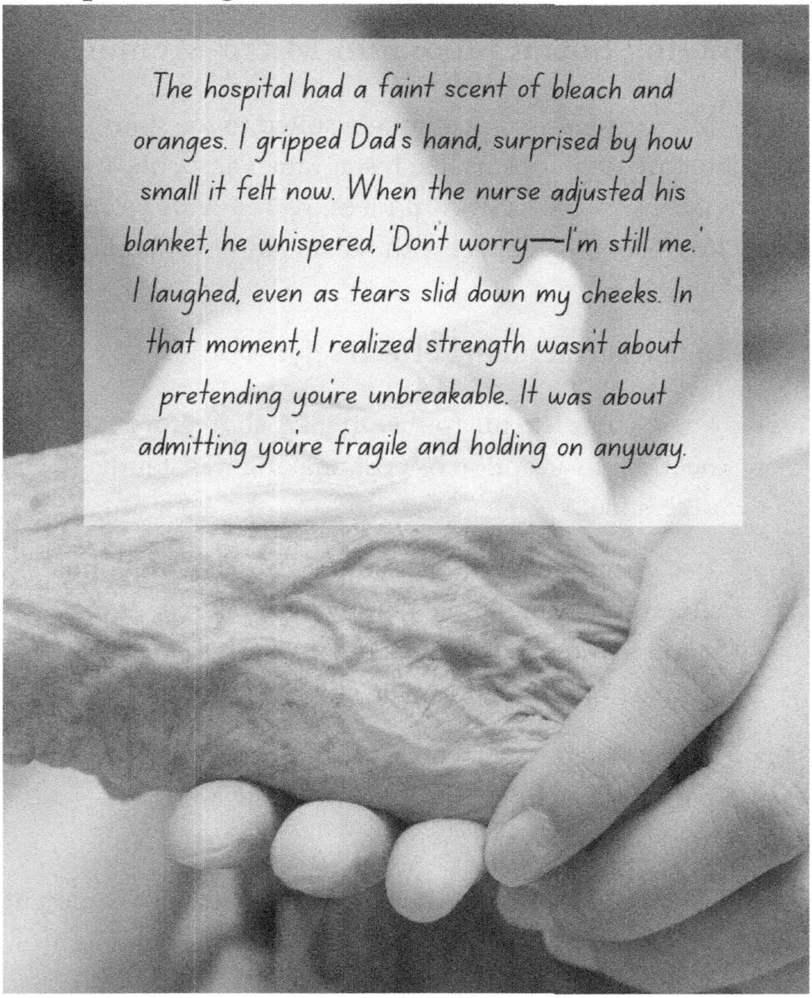

Hashtags: #MicroMemoir #LifeIn150Words #TrueStory #MemoirInMoments

Dealing with Criticism and Rejection

Publishing publicly opens you to feedback—both encouraging and harsh. Here's how to stay grounded:

- Separate You from Your Work: A critique of the writing is not a critique of your worth.
- Look for the Useful Parts: Even painful feedback can highlight where a piece is unclear or underdeveloped.
- Expect Mixed Responses: Some will love your honesty, others will disagree with your choices. That's the nature of memoir.
- Remember Your Purpose: Go back to why you wanted to publish in the first place. That clarity will carry you through.

The Arc in a Compilation

Just like a single micro-memoir, a collection benefits from an arc. Consider:

- Starting Point: Establish your world and your theme.
- Middle: Show the challenges, discoveries, and changes.
- Closing: End with a resolution, insight, or open-ended question that lingers.

Whether your memoir collection is built around recovery from a personal struggle, adapting to a new country, or surviving a high-pressure job, your arc turns it from a set of interesting vignettes into a cohesive, resonant book.

Now Your Turn

From Private Collection to Public Book

1. **Clarify Your Purpose**
    - Why do you want to publish this collection?
        - To inspire?
        - To inform?
        - To preserve a perspective rarely shared?
    - Write a one-sentence mission statement for your book.
2. **Define Your Theme & Arc**
    - Choose a unifying theme (career, cultural experience, recovery, family history, etc.).
    - Sketch your arc: Where does the reader begin, what challenges or discoveries will they witness, and where will they end?
3. **Select Your Strongest Pieces**
    - Pick 20–40 micro-memoirs that fit the theme.
    - Remove or rewrite any that dilute the overall narrative.
4. **Decide Your Publishing Path**
    - Self-publish for full creative control.
    - Hybrid publish if you want some guidance, but will invest financially.

    - Traditional publish if your work fits a publisher's niche and you're willing to query.
    - Experiment with social media platforms.

5. **Plan Your Marketing**
    - Identify 3 audiences most likely to connect with your theme.
    - Brainstorm 5 outreach ideas (events, podcasts, articles, partnerships, social media posts).

6. **Prepare for Feedback**
    - Write three ways you'll remind yourself that critique is about the work, not about you.

📌 **Extra Challenge:** Write your back-cover copy—150 words that introduce your theme, invite curiosity, and hint at your arc. This will help you see your project as a cohesive, publishable book.

Part V

Practice Makes a Story

Chapter 17

50 Micro-Memoir Prompts

Sometimes the hardest part of writing a micro-memoir is deciding *what* to write about. Your life is full of moments—small and large—that could be distilled into a powerful story. The trick is to pick a memory and start capturing it, without worrying yet about whether it's "big enough" or "important enough." Often, the smallest moments hold the deepest meaning.

Below is a list of prompts to help you mine your past for vivid, story-worthy moments. They're organized loosely into themes, but you can start anywhere. Use them for freewriting, warm-ups, or full micro-memoirs.

Firsts

The first time you rode a bike without training wheels.

Your first day at a new school or job.

The first time you cooked a meal on your own.

The first time you broke a bone (or came close).

The first time you stood up to someone.

Lasts

The last time you saw a childhood friend.

The last family holiday in your childhood home.

The last letter or email from someone who's now gone.

The last time you played a sport you once loved.

The last day before a major life change (marriage, move, graduation).

Turning Points

A conversation that completely shifted your opinion.

A moment you realized you were in love.

A day when you decided to quit something.

The moment you recognized your own strength.

A failure that turned out to be a gift.

Family Traditions

A holiday ritual that only your family seems to have.

The "special meal" that marks birthdays or celebrations.

A bedtime story or song passed down through generations.

The yearly trip to a familiar place.

An object that's been in your family for decades.

Accidents & Misadventures

The time you got spectacularly lost.

A cooking disaster that became a running joke.

A travel mishap that turned into a favourite story.

An injury you couldn't help laughing about later.

A party or event that did *not* go as planned.

Private Moments That Changed Everything

A secret you finally told.

The instant you decided to walk away.

A quiet act of kindness that stayed with you.

A personal ritual that brings you comfort.

A moment of joy you never shared—until now.

Childhood Snapshots

A favourite hiding place.

The smell of a season in your hometown.

A beloved toy and its fate.

The neighbour you were a little afraid of. (see chapter 18 for an example)

A game you invented with friends.

Work & School Moments

The teacher who changed your life.

A job you loved but had to leave.

A mistake that taught you something invaluable.

The oddest request you ever got at work.

A co-worker or classmate you'll never forget.

Moments of Awe

The most beautiful place you've ever stood.

A performance that left you speechless.

A sudden encounter with wildlife.

A time you felt truly small under a big sky.

A sound you wish you could hear again.

Unexpected Encounters

Meeting someone famous in the least glamorous place.

A stranger who helped you in a moment of need.

An overheard conversation you'll never forget.

A wrong number that led to something unexpected.

An accidental reunion.

Tip: You can combine these prompts for layered stories. For example, "The first time I stood up to someone" might also be "A turning point" or "A private moment that changed everything."

Pick, Write, Refine

1. **Pick a Prompt**
   - Scan the list of 50 prompts.
   - Circle or mark three that spark a strong emotional pull or vivid image in your mind.
2. **Choose One & Write Freely**
   - Set a timer for 20 minutes.
   - Write your story without editing, censoring, or worrying about grammar. Let it spill out.
3. **Read It Aloud**
   - Reading out loud will help you hear the rhythm, pacing, and emotional beats.
4. **Refine**
   - Ask: Can I make this tighter without losing the heart?
   - Look for one or two sentences that could be more vivid or specific.
5. **Optional Twist**
   - If you wrote 200–300 words, try reducing it to 100 words…then to 50…then to a single sentence. See what happens to the impact as it

shrinks. *Remember: The first version is just the beginning. Each revision teaches you something about your voice and the essence of your story.*

Chapter 18

Memoir Gallery & Annotations

This chapter comprises six micro-memoirs, each accompanied by corresponding annotations.

Wonder Woman on the Loose

The RV trip was a family parade on wheels—two sisters, Mom and Dad, my aunt, uncle, two cousins, and me. Before we left, my parents bought my youngest sister, who was probably around four or five years old at the time, a Wonder Woman bathing suit. Their reasoning was flawless: she was mischievous, and the bright superhero outfit would make her easy to spot.

We rolled into a campsite on a large lake with a sandy beach that stretched for what felt like forever. The air smelled of sunscreen and pine, and the water glittered like it had been sprinkled with sugar. My sister darted toward the shoreline, golden lasso and invisible plane only missing from her costume.

Then—she was gone.

The adults scanned the water first, the way fear tells you to. Dozens of little girls were splashing around in *the exact same bathing suits*. Each time my mom's face lit up with recognition, it fell again. I remember the adults fanning out—my uncle jogging the shoreline, my aunt asking strangers if they'd seen "a Wonder Woman, about this tall."

It felt like hours. In reality, it was probably twenty minutes. My parents had already started weighing the unthinkable when someone shouted from the hill. She'd wandered up to the playground, happily trailing a pack of older kids she'd decided were her new best friends.

Relief came like a wave. The grown-ups laughed shakily, but my sister didn't understand the drama. To her, the day was a triumph: she had played on the swings, made friends, and worn her superhero suit exactly as intended.

Even now, I still can't see Wonder Woman without thinking of the day we almost lost one.

Word Count: 285

Annotation: Wonder Woman on the Loose

- **Sensory details**: Pine scent, glittering water, and sandy beach help root the reader in place.
- **Mid-story turn**: "Then—she was gone." Short sentence for impact.
- **Emotional arc:** Moves from lighthearted to tense to relief, giving a satisfying mini-narrative.
- **Final image:** Links Wonder Woman imagery back to the emotional core, closing the loop.

The Lego Years

The box was almost as big as his torso. His first real Lego set, with a spaceship blazing across the cover, promised adventure. He ripped into the plastic bags, eyes wide, fingers fumbling to snap the bright bricks together.

That afternoon, the kitchen table became a launch pad. Pieces scattered like stardust, instructions bent under eager hands. When the final ship took shape, his grin was so wide it almost eclipsed the creation itself. He didn't just build a toy—he built possibility.

For him, it was joy. For me, it was the beginning of an ongoing truce with the plastic underworld. Lego pieces don't simply fall; they migrate. Across carpets, under couches, into dark corners where the vacuum roars like a predator. They also lie in wait, patient, invisible until a bare foot comes down.

The first time, I thought I had stepped on a shard of glass. The pain was so sharp it made me yelp, sending him into a fit of giggles. After that, I learned to fear the midnight kitchen run, toes curled like a burglar avoiding a booby trap.

Sometimes I crouched to save an expensive specialty block from disappearing into the vacuum bag. Sometimes I swore under my breath, then laughed at myself because what kind of parent wages war against plastic bricks?

He saw magic in every piece. I saw how much I'd pay—for sets, for lost sleep, for the occasional stubbed toe—and how much I'd treasure the sound of them clattering across the floor.

Word Count: 291

Annotation: The Lego Years

- **Opening detail:** "The box was almost as big as his torso," instantly grounds the reader in childhood perspective and scale.
- **Energy in action:** Verbs like "ripped," "fumbling," and "scattered" echo the chaos and excitement of play.
- **Dual lens:** The child's wonder ("built possibility") is contrasted with the parent's practical reality (stepping on Lego, saving blocks from the vacuum).
- **Humour + heart:** The last line reframes inconvenience into love, balancing comedy with sentiment.

The Woman Down the Road

From the prompts: The neighbour you were a little afraid of.

There was something off
about the woman down the road.
Not that she was a single mom,
or that her boys were creepy—
and they were.

It was her eyes,
restless, dark,
like the birch tree that clawed its way
out of a pit in her yard.

She was trusted with us—

morning rides to school,
afternoon rides home—
but I was always leery,
always watching.

One day she snapped,
a brick raised high,
threatening us in our driveway.

The next day,
she died of an aneurysm.

Now I wonder—
was the brick a weapon,
or a flare sent skyward,
a cry we couldn't understand?

How could we have known?

Word Count: 110

Annotation: The Woman Down the Road

- Immediate unease: The opening frames the neighbour as unsettling without explanation, drawing the reader into mystery.
- Symbolism: The birch tree and brick become metaphors for instability and danger.
- Reflection: The ending shifts from childhood fear to adult compassion, deepening the emotional impact.

Wild Raspberries

The sand on the dirt road was like silk—hot silk, warmed all day by the summer sun. We rarely wore shoes, even in the fields. There, we ran barefoot, fast enough that the cut hay only brushed our soles before we escaped its sting.

The air smelled of raspberries, sweet and wild, perfuming the breeze. Their scent was an invitation, pulling us toward the bushes hidden among piled boulders. We searched with stained fingers and sticky lips, believing that no fruit in the world could taste better than these secret treasures we found ourselves. One for me, two for the bowl.

Even now, decades later, the smell of raspberries can carry me back. In an instant, I am barefoot again, the sand soft and hot beneath me, the fields alive with laughter, the world distilled into the taste of sun-warmed fruit.

Word Count: 148

Annotation: Wild Raspberries

- Sensory immersion: Vivid textures ("sand like silk," "cut hay brushed our soles") and smells ("perfumed the breeze") transport the reader directly into the scene, making the memory tangible.
- Childhood authenticity: The barefoot freedom, secret raspberry hunts, and sticky fingers — evokes a child's unfiltered joy, allowing the adult narrator to relive it vividly.
- Reflective resonance: The closing reflection ("Even now… the smell of raspberries can carry me back") ties the sensory detail to the enduring power of memory, showing why small details matter in a life story.

A Brave New World

My mom was thirteen when she stepped off the plane into Canada. She carried only a suitcase, but more striking was what she had left behind: an older sister who chose love over departure, and a country weighed down by arguments that never seemed to end. Ahead of her was a father waiting with a job, a family hoping for a fresh start. The air smelled different; the surrounding voices unfamiliar. Could this new place soften the sharp edges of the past? Could they build a life from loss and arrival, from what they carried—and from what they left behind?

Word Count: 101

Annotation: A Brave New World

- Strong entry point: Opening with "My mom was thirteen" immediately establishes both vulnerability and significance, drawing the reader into a personal yet historic moment.
- Balance of past and future: Juxtaposing what was left behind (sister, arguments, homeland) with what awaited (father, fresh start) frames migration as both loss and possibility.
- Evocative reflection: The closing rhetorical questions give the piece resonance, inviting readers to consider not just one girl's journey, but the universal uncertainty of starting over.

Ninth Grade Limerick

A ninth-grader climbed on the bus,
with no friends to chatter or fuss.

Though her stomach was tight,
she walked halls with her might,
and those walls will soon welcome her trust.

Word Count: 32

Annotation: Ninth Grade Limerick

- Playful tone: The limerick form lightens a serious milestone, showing nerves through rhyme and rhythm rather than heavy description.
- Narrative arc: From nerves and isolation on the bus to courage in the halls, the poem delivers a mini-journey in five lines.
- Hopeful close: The final line reframes anxiety into trust, leaving the reader with optimism about the transition.

Chapter 19

Your Legacy in 300 Words

When you step back and look at the small stories you've captured—whether five or fifty—you'll see more than a collection of moments. You'll see you. Not the resume version. Not the social media highlight reel. The real, messy, tender, and resilient you.

Writing micro-memoirs is an act of both creation and preservation. Each piece is a snapshot in words, a time capsule you can return to. They hold the sights, smells, voices, and emotions that might otherwise fade. They show the arc of your life in fragments—sometimes joyful, sometimes painful, always human.

And here's the beautiful part: you don't need thousands of pages to leave a legacy. A single 300-word piece can carry as much emotional truth as an entire autobiography. You might write yours for a public audience, for your family, or for yourself alone. But in every case, you are capturing something that will outlast the moment.

Micro-memoirs have a way of revealing patterns you didn't know were there. Over time, you may notice recurring themes—your love for water, your instinct to help strangers, your stubborn streak when faced with unfairness. These themes are your threads, woven through your life story. Seeing them laid out can be an unexpectedly powerful form of self-discovery.

Why do these stories matter? Because they remind us that the ordinary is extraordinary when seen through the lens of memory and reflection. They connect us to others. They pass along wisdom, humour, and perspective. They keep the people we've loved—and even the people we've lost—alive in words.

Your legacy isn't measured by the size of your manuscript, but by the truth it carries. And in just 300 words, you can create something timeless.

Your Micro-Memoir Journey

You've explored the many shapes a micro-memoir can take—single sentences, poems, haiku, 300-word arcs. You've learned how to mine your memories, find your voice, capture character, and decide when to go short or long. You've examined your stories from various perspectives and considered how to preserve them for yourself, your family, or the world.

Now it's your turn to take everything you've learned and create a small body of work that reflects you.

Your Final Challenge:

1. **Choose 5–10 moments** that matter to you—mix lighthearted and serious.
2. **Write them in different lengths**—one sentence, 100 words, and 300 words—so you can see how shape changes meaning.
3. **Include at least one past–present lens piece** and one artifact-inspired piece.
4. **Arrange them in an order** that creates a flow—like a personal mixtape of your life.
5. **Read them aloud** or share with someone you trust.

If you want, bind them into a small booklet, print them on cards, post them to a private group, or tuck them away in a box. You've now created something deeply personal and enduring.

Your micro-memoirs don't have to be perfect—they just have to be yours. And the more you write, the richer your legacy will become.

Thank You for Reading

Thank you for joining me on this journey—I'm so grateful for your time and support! Your feedback means a great deal to me, and hearing from readers is one of the most rewarding aspects of being an author. If you enjoyed the book, I'd love it if you could take a moment to share your thoughts in a review on Amazon. Your reviews help other readers discover my work, and I appreciate every word.

If you'd like to reach out directly, feel free to contact me at Kelsey.Pearce.Grit@gmail.com. I'd be delighted to hear from you!

With heartfelt thanks,

Kelsey

Other Works by Kelsey Pearce:

Resiliency and Gratitude Series:

Grateful Grit: Building Resilience Through Gratitude ISBN 978-1738290529

Happiness for the Senses: Mindful Sensory Experience: Taste, Touch, Sight, Smell, Sound ISBN 978-1738290505

Made in United States
North Haven, CT
27 March 2026

90488579R00095